"Harry Willson's previous novel
*magical optimism about humanity. *
a group of cautionary tales and fables, ѕѻʍҽ
others quite absurd. Willson's dissection of human folly is
necessarily painful, but he provides the appropriate general
anaesthetic for the operation: a daring sense of humor.
Definitely recommended."
— Bill Meyers, editor-in-chief, THE STAKE

"Many of the stories are thought-provoking, even
frightening, portrayals of a possible future; nuclear safety,
or the lack thereof, is discussed in several clever scenarios
sketched in real-life terms. 'Peck o' Dirt' is a haunting tale
of progress. 'Duke City Mushroom' does what good
science fiction should do — it creates a story that seems
true but is horrible at the same time. 'Report to Base' has
a great concept/premise. Bill, the alien dog, is a wonderful
character. 'Vermin' is a post-nuclear ANIMAL FARM
where the surviving rodents discuss man's folly, while
dealing with their own."
— Pat Graff, National Teacher of the Year
La Cueva High School, Albuquerque, NM

"Harry Willson confronts head-on the nagging suspicion
many of us have that HOMO SAPIENS is not as sapient as
we pretend, and perhaps not much more than flashes in the
evolutionary pan. His "survival stories" suggest we had
better begin learning from the cockroaches and other
vermin of the earth, if we expect to extend the endgame
being played out on 'our' planet.
"Spinning yarns and parables with spiritual and moral
context, the author skillfully exercises a Socratic method of
questions and conclusions, to expose the truths that the
powers-that-be would rather keep hidden. What other
author doggedly reminds us of how our civilization insists
upon poisoning itself?"
— Jeff Radford, CORRALES COMMENT

"I once thought I was lucky, having been born in August 1944, before the first nuclear bomb explosions. All persons born after July 1945 have strontium-90 in their bones. But I ended up unlucky, too. I joined the Air Force in 1964, to fight in the Vietnam War. A report a few years ago of declassified DOE tests at the Nevada Test Range, where I worked on Air Force weapons programs, reveals that several of the underground tests were 'leakers' which contaminated the area and the people working there.

"Harry Willson's stories are as revealing as the secret DOE reports; he tells us how subtly we are all affected by the nuclear industry. What the DOE would hide from us Harry has placed on paper for all to know, that we are all survivors in one way or another. With the nuclear age our luck has run out, for all of us."

— Bob Anderson, Survivor of Nuclear Contamination

"My dictionary defines vermin as 'any obnoxious or disgusting animal; esp. when difficult to control, as fleas, lice, bedbugs, rats, mice, weasels.' In 'Vermin' I was reminded of Noah and his ark, except that the human species does not survive. It is the pests that confront the problem of survival. The dialogue is delightful.

"The other stories cover a wide spectrum, from the fantastic, 'Something in the Cellar,' to the humdrum domestic 'Rituals,' from modern computers to infertility, from fundamentalism to teen suicide. These are the musings of an agnostic pantheist, who is not above tackling that old philosophical chestnut called, 'free will.'

"Throughout my reading of these stories and pithy comments, the words of Shakespeare's Puck resurfaced again and again: 'What fools these mortals be!'"

— Fred Gillette Sturm, Department of philosophy
University of New Mexico

VERMIN

and Other Survival Stories

Humanity as an Endangered Species

Harry Willson

Illustrated by Claiborne O'Connor

Printed in the United States of America
        First Printing, 1996
        ISBN: 0-938513-22-2
        Library of Congress Catalog Card Number: 96-85282

AMADOR PUBLISHERS
P. O. Box 12335
Albuquerque, NM 87195 USA

Dedicated, with profound thanks for tireless effort, to:

Janet Greenwald
Garland Harris

A royalty of 10% will be divided between:

Citizens for Alternatives to Radioactive Dumping
114 Harvard, SE, Albuquerque, NM 87106

Concerned Citizens for Nuclear Safety
412 W. San Francisco St., Santa Fe, NM 87501

Other books by Harry Willson:

Duke City Tales: Stories from Albuquerque
A World for the Meek: A Fantasy Novel
Souls and Cells Remember: A Love Story
This'll Kill Ya

Other books illustrated by Claiborne O'Connor:

Twelve Gifts: Recipes from a Southwest Kitchen, by Adela Amador
More Gifts, with Variations, by Adela Amador
The Little Brown Roadrunner, by Leon Wender
Duke City Tales, by Harry Willson
This'll Kill Ya, by Harry Willson

Contents

Johnny Plutonium

In our neighborhood there are so many stray dogs, my wife and I can't take our daily walk here. We have to get in the car, pollute the air driving across the river, and go to the park across from the zoo. There we can hike all the way around the football field and the baseball diamond, while keeping the car in sight in the parking lot. I resent not being able to walk in our own neighborhood, and believe I could clear up the matter by carrying and using, when necessary, a baseball bat, but my wife won't hear of it. So we walk near the zoo.

One day we stopped short in our tracks. In front of us, near the end-zone of the empty football field, was a small, well-lettered sign, stapled to a clean wooden stick, which read:

Plutonium Pu

In front of the sign was a little mound of pale brownish crystals. We walked around, but said nothing, to anybody.

The next day, the sign was gone.

The day after that, there was a YAF game about to get under way, when we arrived for our walk. Youngsters, too young for such violent blocking and tackling in my opinion, were ready to play supervised, refereed, cheer-led football. But the game was not getting under way.

Parents of the youngsters were screaming at two young men in black-and-white striped shirts. "Well, *do* something!" "Call the *police!*" "Get it outa here!" "I'm not letting my boy play in *that* stuff!"

We were able to get close enough to see that the plutonium sign was in place, behind another little pile of crystals.

"I don't think it *is* plutonium!" one young father yelled. "I read that plutonium is *white!* This stuff is brown. It looks just like sand."

"Yeah, but how do you know? How does anybody know?" a

1

young mother asked.

"Call the police! Call the F.B.I.!" More and more parents took up that cry.

We resumed our walk, and the game still hadn't started when we finished our two laps around the entire park.

The crowd was near panic, when we drove away. We found nothing in the newspaper, or the TV news about the incident.

On subsequent hikes we found more little plutonium signs at different locations in the park, and on one occasion noticed one on the picnic table beside the swings and rides set up for toddlers.

Then stories did hit the papers. YAF games were canceled, or rescheduled. Some parents pulled their boys out of the league. Teams from the affluent north-east heights refused to play teams from the valley, where the zoo is located.

The city council saw fit to issue a press release to the media. "There is no loose plutonium in Duke City," it said. "Someone with a sick mind is placing signs that say, 'Plutonium,' in city parks, for unknown reasons. It is a sort of terrorism. Plutonium is nothing to be afraid of. There is no plutonium in Duke City."

Plutonium signs have been found at the university soccer field, as well as other valley parks. A popular song has been written, and played on local radio, called, "Plutonium in the Grass."

For some weeks we saw no more signs on our walks at the zoo. Then one day two police cars, with lights flashing, were in the parking lot and two police officers stood near the picnic table. When we approached, it became clear that they were questioning an elderly gentleman, who sat on the bench smiling benignly at the policemen. "Surely it's not a crime to sit on a park bench, Gentlemen," he was saying. He looked each policeman in the eye, one after the other.

"Are these yours?" the older of the two officers asked, waving his hand at several baggies on the table. Each one contained some pale brown crystals.

"They're my gift to the sovereign people," the man answered

cheerfully.

"So, they *are* yours," the policeman insisted.

"Well, not really," the man answered. "Not any more."

"Did you bring them here?"

"Yes, I did."

"What's that stuff in 'em?" the younger policeman asked gruffly. "Where'd you get 'em?"

"I got the material on the West Mesa. It's called 'blow sand,'" the old man replied. His white hair was ruffled, but he was not. I marvelled at how calm he was.

"Blow sand! Why are you labeling it 'Plutonium'?"

"In order to raise the consciousness of the sovereign citizens of Duke City."

"Do you know what plutonium even *is?*" the older policeman asked. He also sounded out of patience.

"I do," the old man replied, "although most of the sovereign citizens do not. It is a man-made substance, designed to cause extremely destructive explosions. It is radioactive and lethal, causing cancer in the lungs and on the skin of those who come into contact with it. It remains lethal for more than a quarter of a million years. One half-life of plutonium is twenty-five thousand years, which is more than twice the age of human civilization —"

"I don't need a lecture," the policeman interrupted.

"I'm very glad of that," the old man said. "Most of the sovereign citizens do." We were amazed at his calm manner, and so were the police. They seemed to think he should be afraid of them, and he was not.

The younger officer said to the other, "I think we should run him in. He's been causing panic, disturbing the peace, to say the least. We might even make a terrorism charge stick."

"How can telling the truth be called terrorism?" the old man asked.

"*Truth?*" the older cop yelped. "It's blow sand and you call it plutonium, and you want us to call that truth?"

"But it is true that there is plutonium in the grass here." The old man waved his hand out over the outfield of the baseball diamond.

"Who says so?" the younger policeman barked. He turned to the older officer and said, "I still think we should run him in, Sir."

"Radioactive waste, including plutonium, is allowed into the sewer system, by vote of the City Council," the old man said patiently.

"Well, they have to do something with it," the older cop said. He was more interested in the old man's ideas than the younger one, who seemed to want tough action without thinking about it.

"They do, indeed," the man said to the older policeman. "No one yet knows what to do with it. Putting it in the sewer, where it is gone out into the world, or burying it in the ground, where it cannot be retrieved and will end up out in the world — there are several things they ought *not* to do with it. They also ought not to sprinkle it on the strawberries, or put it in the green chile stew."

The man and the older cop smiled at each other. "So what about the sewer," the cop asked.

"The sludge from the sewage treatment plant has been spread on the grass of the public parks as fertilizer. It contains plutonium and other radioactive substances, which have been detected by the scientists at the Special Weapons Lab. The report was made public, but never publicized. So here am I, with my little attempt at consciousness-raising. I'm willing to publicize the truth that has been kept hidden."

"Sir," the younger officer said, "he's been spreading panic."

"Truth leads to panic sometimes," the old man said. "Depending on how it is taken. Truth will not remain hidden forever. Truth will out. When the young ball-players develop lung cancer, perhaps some years from now, truth will out." The old man stared from one policeman's face to another.

"Shall I cuff him, Sir?" the younger cop asked.

"For what?" the old man asked mildly. "Spreading truth? You'll cause more panic than I have yet caused."

"I'm going to call headquarters," the older policeman announced.

"Yes," the old man said, a little eagerly. "Call the mayor. Call the TV stations. Call the editors of the newspapers."

My wife had been pulling on my arm persistently for some time, wanting to get away, before anything violent erupted. I let her drag me away, and when I looked back, the three were still talking earnestly.

◇　◇　◇

The Leukemia Question

A group of us, concerned about the government's plans to seal the fate of our state by making it the Nuclear Sacrifice Zone, announced a public demonstration at the office of our local congressman in downtown Duke City. A new bill had been proposed in Congress, which would exempt the Waste Isolation Pilot Project, called WIPP, from nuclear waste safety requirements and independent oversight. WIPP is the proposed repository for the "transuranic waste" generated by the production of nuclear weapons.

Our media committee did its job, and for a brief period there were almost as many television reporters and camera-persons present as protestors. Some demonstrators carried signs that insisted that the Environmental Protection Agency and not the Department of Energy supervise the question of safety at the repository.

WE DEMAND EPA OVERSIGHT

WIPP IS NOT SAFE

CHECK DOE SAFETY RECORD

WIPP = CHERNOBYL

Other demonstrators carried more enigmatic signs.

GROUND ZERO

TRAIL OF BROKEN TREATIES

6

YOU CAN'T HUG CHILDREN WITH NUCLEAR ARMS

THE ENEMY WITHIN

The TV cameras were concentrating on the leaders of our group, near the entrance to the office building. We protestors marched with our signs in front of the door, and then on down the block to the corner of the next street. At that point we wheeled around, turned our signs to face the street and the cameras, and paced back to a point beyond the entrance, where we turned around again and marched back.

After several marches back and forth on the sidewalk, I noticed a newcomer to the scene, standing at the corner of the building, leaning on the wall, with a sign over his head. I motioned to him to get in our line ahead of me, but he shook his head, "No." A boy of about eight years of age stood close to him. His refusal to join us puzzled me, until I read his sign, on the next walk-around. It said simply, "Support WIPP."

I stepped out of line and approached him. "You support WIPP?" I asked.

He appeared frightened; his eyes were open wide, and he looked away from me as soon as I established eye contact. He bobbed his head up and down, once, as if to say, "Yes."

I studied the boy standing next to him. He also looked afraid. It was obvious that neither of them had ever before exercised their constitutional right to assemble and demand redress of grievances. They were part of that vast majority who aren't sure that the guarantee of that right is a good idea.

"Are you from here?" I asked. Those of us who do value that right use it in more than one area of concern, and thus come to know each other and recognize each other. I was sure that I had never seen him before.

He shook his head, "No."

A light came on in my mind. "Ah! You're from Carlsbad." That's the town near where the Department of Energy has spent one billion dollars preparing the proposed nuclear waste repository. He nodded, "Yes." More than ninety percent of the residents of that county say they favor WIPP, when polled.

"You never watched a kid die of leukemia, did you?" I asked. His eyes bugged open wider, but he did not speak. "I did," I told him. "It was very unpleasant, even for me, let alone for her."

The boy standing next to the counter-protestor touched the man's arm and said, "Dad —"

"It was a mess," I continued. "It took a long time, too. It started as a nosebleed that wouldn't stop. Then it made her skin very shiny and clear — you thought you could see right through it. Then little blood clots appeared under the thin shiny surface of the skin. Then her cheeks swelled up, but they said that was from the medicine."

The boy said again, "Dad —"

I went on. "They took her to surgery and removed her spleen, without ever explaining why they thought that would help."

"You're bothering me," the man said. It was the first time he spoke.

"I'm trying to," I said. "She became very tender and loving, very fragile and precious. She wrote poems, telling how much she loved us all, and how she was going to a place where everything was perfect, and she was not very sad about that, just about leaving us all behind."

"You're bothering me," the man repeated.

"The whole experience cost me my faith," I said. "I was no longer able to believe that a good and all-powerful God was in charge of the world. But I still believe that we have to love each other, and our children, even if there isn't any God to guarantee anything. We have to protect them as best we can."

"They told me not to let anyone bother me, and you're bothering me," the man said.

"How much are they paying you to come here and hold that sign in the middle of our demonstration?" I asked.

He did not reply.

"I realize that you don't think that's any of my business, but you know, it really is, since I and all these people, and all the taxpayers are furnishing that money."

"Don't bother me," the man said.

"I've come to believe in love and truth, and that's why I'm here, and then I find you here, who believe only in money. Are they paying your boy?" I looked the boy in the face. He looked terrified.

"You don't want this boy of yours to get leukemia. Believe me, you don't. I suspect that you don't understand what 'half-life' even means. You may not believe that plutonium causes leukemia. Maybe you never even heard of leukemia before today. You believe the lies that the DOE teaches. You don't understand how much time two hundred and fifty thousand years even is, how much leukemia and how much suffering that means for future generations. People like you, who believe in money instead of truth and love, don't care about future generations much, I've noticed — but you don't want your boy to get leukemia. Believe me, you don't."

Our group continued to march back and forth in front of the door of the local office of the congressman. Our leaders were inside, trying to talk to him. Each marcher looked at the three of us standing on the corner, as they made their about-face. I did not rejoin them, but stood like a sentinel beside the frightened man whose sign said that he supported WIPP. My sign said,

GROUND ZERO.

The boy pulled on his father's arm and said, "Let's go, Dad." One more time the man said to me, "You're bothering me."

"Good," I said, and then held my tongue.

The man lowered his sign, and he and the boy turned the corner and walked rapidly away from all of us.

◇   ◇   ◇

Peck o' Dirt

Erin and Shelby found Grandpa out front, with a plastic grocery bag half full. "Watcha got there, Grandpa?" Shelby asked. She was the younger granddaughter.

"Today's trash," Grandpa replied. His cheerful voice told the girls he was glad to see them, but the disgust he felt toward the litter he had gathered came through at the same time. "The people walking and driving by drop it. I pick up a peck every couple of days," he added.

"A peck o' trash? What's a peck, Grandpa?" Shelby asked.

"It's — " Grandpa started to answer, but Erin interrupted.

"It's an old-fashioned word, meaning a certain amount. How much is it, Grandpa? This much?" Erin held out her hands, palms toward each other.

"Well, I didn't know the word was antiquated already," he answered. "A peck is one quarter of a bushel." He grinned. "But you don't know what a bushel is, either, do you? Bushel baskets aren't as common as they used to be."

"Is it *that* much?" Erin asked, pointing at the bag in Grandpa's hand, almost full of papers, plastic cups, large paper cups, bottles, cans, cigarette wrappers, plastic strips and other bits of discarded packaging material.

"Just about," he answered. "I'd call this about a peck. Good word — 'peck.' We used to use it all the time, when I was a kid. F'rinstance, in the phrase, 'peck o' dirt.'"

"What does *that* mean?" Shelby asked.

By this time they had walked around to the back of the house. They sat on a bench and looked out over Grandpa's back yard. "Whenever a kid pulled a carrot from the garden, he'd rub it on

10

his pants a little and then bite off the end. Then he, or maybe one of the other kids around, would say, 'Peck o' dirt.' We all knew it referred to the old idea that everyone eats a peck o' dirt a year. So, this kid was getting a little of his peck with his carrot."

Shelby grinned, but Erin had a face which said she didn't like this story. Grandpa went on.

"Sometimes, not every time, but once in a while, the chewer of the unwashed carrot would spit out all the contents of his mouth, and say, 'Peck o' dirt! But I don't want to eat all of mine in one day!' And we'd all laugh. It was silly, I guess. A kind of game we had."

Shelby was grinning, but Erin turned on her and stated, very forcefully, "It's a stupid story! Don't you try anything like that! Don't you dare eat dirt. You wash what you eat first. And peel it!"

Grandpa said something about "clean dirt," but Erin would have none of it. She was really steamed up.

"There's no such thing! Not any more. I mean it, Shelby. There's poison in the ground. Don't you dare eat it!"

"Poison?" Shelby asked.

"Yes, poison," Erin insisted. "Gasoline, crankcase oil, brake fluid, battery acid! Who knows what all?"

Grandpa remembered at that point that the girls lived in a fancy tract house that had been built over a landfill that the city had taken almost ten years to fill. Who, indeed, knows what all might be in the soil of any garden they'd plant on *that* lot?

Erin was raving on. "Cow manure and horse manure might be what Grandpa would call 'clean dirt.' We have photography chemicals, pesticides, paint with lead in it, *plutonium!* A peck o' that stuff will do us *all* in, in no time. Don't you go around eating dirt!" She yelled at Shelby, "Maybe it was a safe thing to do fifty years ago, but it is not safe now! Tell her, Grandpa."

He was startled. "Tell her?"

"Tell her not to do what *you* did, Grandpa."

Grandpa looked at the sisters and felt sad. Clean dirt — one more thing destroyed by "progress."

  "Yeah, Shelby," he said finally. "Your sister Erin is right. Don't eat any dirt. I'm sorry I brought it up." He swung the plastic bag of trash back and forth between his legs as he sat on the bench, staring at his garden.

◊   ◊   ◊

Too Cheap to Meter

First I find myself astonished, and then depressed, by the newspaper review of a book, recently released by a big-name publisher, in which a Ph.D.-wielding employee of the Department of Energy, tells how the nation is not going to be able to continue to delay building new nuclear reactors with which to generate electricity. The author dismisses all alternatives as "worse." He never mentions conservation of electricity and limitation of population growth and massive life-style change as possible alternatives. But what drove me to the word-processor was the assertion that "no one has ever been injured by what the media have called 'nuclear accidents,' such as Three Mile Island." The author seems content to ignore leukemia rates in key counties across the nation, including Los Alamos, NM, Hanford, WA, and Savannah River, SC.

I sent the following "guest editorial" to the local newspaper:

"The Department of Energy does not know what to do with the nuclear waste created by the nuclear weapons industry and the nuclear power plant industry. So in order to pretend to be doing something with it, the DOE proposes burying it. The first test-site for this burial program is The Waste Isolation Pilot Project, abbreviated WIPP, near Carlsbad, New Mexico.

"One of DOE's most urgent arguments for 'opening WIPP,' i.e. beginning to truck transuranic waste from twenty-three states to New Mexico before safety standards are met, or even defined, is that they have already spent over one billion dollars digging the facility, and paying 'scientists' to testify falsely at public safety hearings. We need to continue to ponder costs.

"Plutonium causes lung cancer and leukemia. It needs to be guarded, even if safely buried, to keep people from coming into

13

contact with it. What would the total cost be for one 24-hour-a-day 'guardianship?' There are hundreds of thousands of tons of this stuff — **every** operating nuclear power plant turns into 'nuclear waste' at the end of thirty years — all the pipes and gauges, and all the concrete. We will need several guardianships, several thousand, several dozen thousand. Let's calculate how much *one* will cost.

"24 hours a day. 365.25 days per year equals 8766 hours per year. At minimum wage, say $5.00 an hour, that's $43,830 per year, with no provision for 'benefits' for the workers.

"DOE promises to keep the nuclear waste 'safe' for 10,000 years. To pretend that any promise can be meaningful for that long is blatantly preposterous, but let's continue our arithmetic. These are the new 'written problems' our fifth graders should be learning to solve. $43,830 per year for 10,000 years equals $438,300,000 for one guardianship.

"Plutonium remains lethal for 250,000 years. The half-life is 25,000 years. If we're really going to keep it 'safe,' that's how long we have to keep it. $43,830 per year for 250,000 years, assuming that our leaders really do have inflation under control equals $10,957,500,000. That's more than ten times the amount already spent on the first hole in the ground, of which there will have to be dozens.

"Has this arithmetic ever been done before? This stuff is not 'too cheap to meter.' It's too expensive to comprehend. No wonder the power companies leave the problem of nuclear waste disposal out of all their cost analyses.

"Does this arithmetic at least suggest that we do not need to make any more of this material, for weapons or for electricity?"

I never received any response from the editor of the paper, and never saw in print my attempt to contribute to the discussion.

◊   ◊   ◊

Another Lottery

The recent earthquake in southeastern New Mexico and west Texas has demolished the downtown areas of several mid-sized towns, including Carlsbad, NM and Pecos, TX. The Department of the Interior has closed the Carlsbad Caverns National Park to the public, while a team of seismologists assesses the damage to the caverns.

A very serious casualty of the earthquake is the Waste Isolation Pilot Project, a facility on which the Department of Energy has spent more than one billion dollars, preparing a depository for the nuclear waste which is generated by the process of manufacturing nuclear warheads. The waste was to be shipped to New Mexico from the "points of origin," in Washington, Idaho, Colorado, Ohio, South Carolina, Tennessee and other places in New Mexico.

The salt beds which were to encapsulate the waste have collapsed completely, and a source of brine, which had previously been regarded as minor, has been exposed, making the site useless. "Our earth-moving machinery is completely useless. It's as if we had never started digging," one worker stated.

◇ ◇ ◇

The eruption of Quartzite Mountain in Nevada has interfered with very little civilized activity. No towns of any size and very few public roads have been affected. The exception is the obliteration of Yucca Mountain, a repository designed to hold the radioactive waste from the nation's electricity-generating nuclear power plants. Several billion dollars had already been invested in the site, which was to become the final resting place for every decommissioned nuclear power plant in the nation.

15

◇   ◇   ◇

What has become known as The Nuclear Sacrifice Zone Debate is now raging from the floors of Congress in Washington to the town halls and editorial pages of the entire nation.

"We must make a selection openly and fairly. The previous plans were arbitrary and politically motivated, and could never be guaranteed safe. Now Mother Nature has scrapped them, and we must start over."

In previous debates and testimony, some persons, especially those from the area around Carlsbad, NM, indicated that they were more interested in some kind of economic lift from the project than in any possible increase in the leukemia rate. That point of view, now called "the jobs-at-any-price" angle, is not being offered in current discussion. "NIMBY" is now everyone's attitude — "not in my back yard." "We don't want to become the nation's nuclear cess pool."

The long-time practice of the government, according to which the people of the United States were regarded as the real enemy to be lied to, and poisoned by radioactive substances, and taxed in order to pay for the lies and the poison has been abandoned. "Classified," meaning, "to be kept secret," was a method of keeping secrets from the "sovereign" American taxpayer, more than from any external enemy, but no longer.

"The great flaw in all the reasoning and planning and spending up to this point can be seen in the following analogy. If a careless, thoughtless, mindless, unaware person leaves the faucet running, and the water runs unchecked for a very long period, flooding the floor, filling the basement, destroying the contents of the house, flooding the neighborhood, the first thing that must be done, before an effective clean-up can be undertaken, is to *turn off the faucet!*

"We are creating a huge quantity of extremely dangerous material, material which will be lethal to our descendants for ten thousand generations. This verges on the unimaginable but is in no way an exaggeration.

"When the people of the United States figure this out, it will then become necessary to shut down *all* nuclear facilities, to forswear the use of nuclear weapons altogether, and to make electricity some other way. All the nuclear facilities, military and electric, are unsafe, and create by-products which are lethal and will remain lethal for hundreds of thousands of years."

◇   ◇   ◇

The Nuclear Sacrifice Zone debate took a new turn recently when a nation-wide forum of scientists recommended taking the question away from politicians. "Repositories can be, and have been, forced down the throats of states which cannot defend themselves. In the past, congressional delegations have been purchased wholesale, and cheap, by the Department of Energy and the nuclear industry. The only fair thing would be to conduct a lottery. Which state shall be sacrificed?

"Place fifty counters in the Bingo machine. There would probably be less unpleasant complaining afterward if it took forty-nine draws to eliminate all but one, instead of letting the first draw decide.

"Americans have used the lottery before to decide things, for example, when nothing more serious than individual 19-year-old male lives were at stake. Who shall be sent to Vietnam to be shot? There is also Biblical precedent. Many ancient cultures believed it was a way to let God, or the gods, decide difficult and unpleasant matters. We could do the same.

"In honor of the sacrificed state we could color one of the fifty stars on the flag black. We could leave empty seats and desks in the meeting halls of Congress, to remind us of what our foolishness has cost.

"Or, perhaps better, we could divide the land mass into fifty equal-sized, roughly rectangular units, except for irregular coastlines, and ignore state boundaries. Then conduct the lottery to see which chunk will have to be sacrificed. Geological considerations will hardly be necessary, really, when we begin to take into account the full time in which this material is lethal.

"The government has promised to keep this material 'safe' for ten thousand years. Ten thousand years ago agriculture had not yet been invented. But ten thousand years is not what we're dealing with here. The half-life of plutonium is 25,000 years, meaning any quantity of it will still be lethal after 250,000 years. Anything can happen anywhere geologically in 250,000 years.

"So, the lottery decides where. Move everybody out. Excavate. Build lead walls and a lead floor around and under it. Move all the nuclear by-product material, all the bombs, all the barrels and boxes of contaminated material, all the dismantled nuclear facilities — to that place. Dump it in there. Put a lead and concrete seal over it. Put up signs that say, 'Do not enter. Do not touch. Do not drill. Do not dig. Do not mine. Do not explore. Do not be curious about what is in here — "in the day that you touch it you shall surely die..."' — and hope it holds, including the language the signs are written in, for two hundred and fifty thousand years.

"It will be expensive. At the moment we are setting aside over $300 billion a year, just in one department, which will be available for this task as soon as we become clear as to who or what 'the enemy' is. This poison problem is the biggest and the most implacably dangerous enemy we have. The longer we refuse to admit it, and refuse to shut off the flow in order to stop enlarging it, the less likely it becomes that we will ever be able to get rid of it."

The debate rages on, with no firm decision to report as yet.

◊   ◊   ◊

Duke City Mushroom

Several local roto-rooter businesses have reported a strange phenomenon in the sewer lines of private homes, in various sections of the city. They indicate that their rotating blade normally cuts through elm tree roots, trumpet vine roots, and any other kind of obstruction short of hardened concrete. Now they and their equipment are completely stymied by a substance in the line, which allows itself to be cut up by the blades, but is not removed, or affected in any perceptible way, by such action. The lines remain clogged. When the lines are dug up, and the sewer pipes completely replaced, the problem seems to be taken care of. The old pipes are full of a thick gelatinous brown mass, which does not let water, or anything else, pass through.

◊ ◊ ◊

After a recent article in *THE NEW AGE JOURNAL,* describing what was cleverly called, "The Fungus Among Us," this reporter contacted the proprietor of a local bookstore for additional information. The man stated that he has heard of several thriving businesses in Southern California which sell "the mushroom." He himself went to Los Angeles to investigate, but decided that the whole idea was simply more evidence that Southern California, like Santa Fe, has gone mad. He called it "La-la Land." "New Age entrepreneurs multiply like toadstools in the night, offering one scam after another to the gullible," he reported. "Some businesses sell 'starter kits' for $50 each. I watched the proprietors talking to what looked like lined-up bowls of tea." The man rolled his eyes at me, and turned that little invisible crank beside his right ear.

◊ ◊ ◊

Our reporter has located some local aficionados of the

Siberian mushroom, sometimes called also the Manchurian mushroom, and filed this report.

The name of the mushroom is Kombucha. Actually it isn't a mushroom at all, but a symbiotic colony of yeast and bacteria. But everyone into this new craze calls it a mushroom. Half a cup of tea, in which this thing has been growing at room temperature for a week, taken on an empty stomach upon arising every morning, is supposed to provide longevity and extra energy. It is said to strengthen the immune system and offer relief from the symptoms of assorted ailments, ranging from diabetes to arthritis. One unsubstantiated claim states that it can cure AIDS, by its effect on the immune system.

"My energy level is notably higher."

"I keep last week's mushroom on my desk in a saucer, and rub my swollen arthritic knuckle on it from time to time. The swelling has gone down, and the pain has gone completely. The mushroom is like a companion at my desk."

"This is a little crude to talk about, on radio, maybe. But its effect on me is that once a day I feel that my lower digestive tract is clear, emptied *out* altogether, cleaned out. I'm not sitting on, or carrying around, several pounds of mildly poisonous fecal matter that my body is finished with already. That is gone out of there."

"Where'd we get it? From the University. Yes, I know that sounds unlikely. From the Arts and Sciences Department. Every counsellor and secretary in the office there has tried this mushroom. We got it from someone we know who works there."

"We have given several away, but don't know of anyone who has taken the tea for as long as we have — more than fifteen months. We are older and wiser, quite alert and in excellent health, with no interference from the professional medical establishment. Maybe we would have been anyway, but then again, maybe not."

"Sure, I'll tell you how to make the tea. You boil three cups of water with one cup of light brown sugar. We do that in a glass bowl in the microwave, since metal does bad things to the tea and to the mushroom and to the human drinkers of the tea. I remove the staple from a family-size tea-bag, and retie it, and steep that for half an hour. We put the three quarts of sugar/tea in a plastic container, with the mushroom, after the tea has cooled. We know someone who killed the mushroom, putting it into boiling water.

"The mushroom floats near the surface. We cover it, very loosely, with a lid. Over a period of a week, the mushroom "digests" the tea and sugar, producing a film on the surface, thin at first, but thickening as the week wears on. When we redo the process, a week later, a new mushroom has formed on the surface, easily separated from the old one. We take the container of tea, strain it, and keep it in the refrigerator. We make a new batch of tea and place the new mushroom in it. The old one can be given to someone else who wants to do this, or it can be thrown away, not into the sewer, or the septic tank system. We put ours in the compost pile."

"No, I don't think persons should sell it, or buy it. It is a gift from Nature, and should be passed from person to person as a gift."

◇   ◇   ◇

We have asked the president of the local American Medical Association for an evaluation of the safety and medical effects of the Kombucha mushroom. It does seem to be a growing thing here in Duke City, doesn't it, Doctor?

"The medical community is alarmed, if this really is as widespread as your reports and others seem to indicate. The substances produced by such an uncontrolled process could be extremely dangerous. No, it's not similar to home-made beer; that's an entirely different thing. People are pretending that this has a medical function. They're taking this 'tea,' instead of seeking professional medical help for their health problems. The anecdotal stories of people benefitting from this are totally unconvincing and irrelevant. People have no business feeling healthy and energetic without our involvement. Think of the jobs that would be lost, if the general population discovered that they don't need our permission to be healthy and happy!

"It really is a dire situation. The spores of deadly bacteria could get into that culture medium and do great harm. I hope no one is giving it to babies, or weakened elderly people. I can only encourage sensible people to stop this foolishness at once. It should be regulated, and made illegal."

◊   ◊   ◊

City authorities, after avoiding our questions for several days, are now admitting that there is serious trouble at the sewage treatment plant on South Second Street. What seemed to be a local phenomenon, at several individual homesites, has now become very serious at the plant. A strange brown substance clogs the lines coming into the plant. Sewage has backed up into many homes near the plant. Main arteries from other sections of town have been diverted and now empty directly into the river, because the lines leading into the plant are clogged and can't be opened. The odor, which could already be detected in mild form on certain days, called bad-air days, now permeates at all times the entire south side of town. The river stinks all the way to Belen.

Authorities are not sure of the cause of this disaster. Some suspect something alive growing in the sewer. Some citizens have raised again the question of secrecy regarding certain chemical/biological experiments at various hospitals in town, conducted under the auspices of the Department of Defense. Others wonder about the radioactivity which is dumped into the sewer every hour of the day and night, with the permission of the City Council, by hospitals and the Special Weapons Laboratory at the Base located in the southeast heights.

◊   ◊   ◊

Reporters have visited the sewage treatment plants, equipped with gasmasks and cameras. They report a huge brown amorphous mass, oozing up and over and around the holding tanks. It seems to be growing in size. It glows at night, raising the question of radioactivity in the sewer. Police have cordoned off the area, labelling it a crime scene, although it attracts very

few visitors, because of the odor. Private citizens have reported
that even at the barricades their amateur Geiger counters click
madly and the needle is off the scale.

◇   ◇   ◇

Garbage workers returning from the landfill south of town
report that another brown blob is growing there. It absorbs all
organic matter, including plastic bags. It is growing at an
alarming rate, they state.

University chemists and biologists visited the site and report
that the blob is a colony of yeast and bacteria, mutated probably
from the so-called Kombucha mushroom. It is now mildly
radioactive, having picked up plutonium which enters the landfill
in the groundwater leaching down from the Special Weapons
Laboratory in the southeast heights.

◇   ◇   ◇

There are two growing masses in the South Valley east of the
River. One began at the sewage treatment plant on South Second
Street. The other began at the landfill, now closed, south of Rio
Bravo. These masses are similar in their voracious appetite for
organic matter. Sewage is mostly organic. Much of the material
at the landfill is organic, in spite of pleas to citizens to learn
composting. Both masses concentrate whatever radioactivity they
encounter. The Sewage Plant Blob contains a great variety of
isotopes. The Landfill Blob is predominantly plutonium, which
has a half-life of 25,000 years.

The Sewage Plant Blob has reached the River. The additional
moisture seems to accelerate its growth process, and it appears
to be filtering into itself the radioactivity that is in the River,
from Los Alamos and from the leaking sewage treatment plant
itself.

◇   ◇   ◇

Local disciples of the Kombucha mushroom report their
continued use of the tea, which supposedly enhances health and
a sense of well-being, in spite of the growing opposition of the
American Medical Association, locally and nationally.

"We were advised not to put the old mushrooms in the sewer,

but evidently someone got careless," one anonymous user reports.

◇   ◇   ◇

The City Council has declared the mushroom, and its tea, to be illegal substances. It is now illegal to sell, give away, or own the mushroom, or drink the tea. No plans for enforcement have yet been announced.

◇   ◇   ◇

The Air Force has attacked the two blobs, fearing what could happen if the two masses meet. Radioactivity is being concentrated in both of them, and questions of critical mass have arisen. Some experts have thought an explosion could result. One said his calculations indicated the possibility of igniting the atmosphere itself.

An effective means of military attack has not yet been devised. There is no brain, and no nervous system, in the enemy. Rifles, machine guns, howitzers, bombs, nerve gas, B-2 bombers, anti-craft carriers, computerized simulated night-vision super-weapons — all are evidently useless.

One anonymous user of the Kombucha mushroom called to suggest boiling water. "I killed one that way," she reported. The City Council, the state governor and the Air Force have all rejected the proposal, saying, "It would be too expensive." Meanwhile, real estate prices are down, and revenue from tourism has plummeted, in Duke City.

◇   ◇   ◇

Stop the Machine

It was early summer and very hot. Thorne was in shorts and shirt-sleeves, and a jaunty straw hat. The dry heat is bearable, he thought to himself as he walked from his car to the downtown library, as long as you stay in the shade, or carry your shade with you. That's why they call a hat a *sombrero* — it's a shade-maker.

Thorne found what he wanted in the reference section, sat at one of the long tables and went to work. His concentration was broken after some minutes, when he glanced at his own bare arm and saw the white hairs standing at full attention. He then noticed for the first time that his leg was jiggling up and down rapidly. He felt thoroughly chilled.

He got up and went to the librarian's desk. "How cold is it in here?" he asked the young woman, who had a heavy wool sweater draped across her shoulders.

"I don't know," she said, smiling sweetly. She poked one arm and then the other into the sleeves of her sweater, and shrugged it on properly. "But it seems cold to me."

"I'm freezing," Thorne said. "It's the month of June, and ninety-five degrees out there."

"I know."

"Where's the thermostat?" Thorne asked.

"Oh, I have no idea. That's taken care of downstairs."

"You're the chief librarian?"

"Yes, Sir." She smiled more sweetly than ever.

"You're in charge of all the books, and who checks out what, and all that, but you can't regulate the temperature?"

"Building maintenance does that," she explained. "I've called down already, but no one has answered yet."

"It seems to me the city is setting a very bad example," Thorne said. "You want us to conserve energy, and yet you waste it, making it uncomfortably cold in June."

"I agree. It isn't in my control, however."

"You can't just turn it off?" Thorne asked.

"No, Sir. I have no idea how to do that."

Thorne drove to the supermarket, planning to pick up several items. By the time he arrived at the check-out line, the hairs on his arms were standing on end again. The checkers were wearing heavy warm-up jackets, zipped up to the neck, with the hoods covering their ears. "Why doesn't the manager turn it down, or off?" Thorne asked the woman who was sacking his items.

"He doesn't know how. He's put in a call, but nobody has come yet."

Thorne went to visit his father at the nursing home. He noticed that all the residents were huddled in chairs wrapped in heavy blankets, or in bed. Aides were hustling down the hall with piles of blankets. "You wouldn't have to charge us three thousand a month, if you got your energy costs under control," Thorne stated at the business desk.

"We can't understand it. The building maintenance crew has turned the thermostat up as high as it will go, but they can't get the machine to shut off."

On the way home Thorne recalled a story he had read ages ago, futuristic sci-fi stuff, by E. M. Forster, of all people. All the inhabitants lived and worked in individual cubicles in a sort of underground hive. Food was provided, and the air and temperature were controlled by machine. Very few persons had ever visited the surface. They were all content to live and work inside. One could hear the machine, humming very gently all the time. There was no day, no night, no summer, no winter — the machine took care of everything.

It was a horror story, Thorne remembered. "The Machine Stops." Yes. And when it stopped, our hero had to do something. Find a way out, rediscover the surface, adapt to reality.

That evening the local news media told their stories but did not pick up on the real news of the day. Most people, including reporters and producers of news shows, thought the cold was caused by local mechanical phenomena, confined to whatever buildings they were in. Tellers had trouble counting money in banks. Oil flowed annoyingly slowly at car repair shops. Holy water froze in the fonts of the large churches.

By the third day it was generally known that all air conditioners in the city were out of order. Public buildings were affected: court houses, police stations, jails, libraries, community centers. Private business was affected: retail stores, lawyers' offices, for-profit hospitals and nursing homes, taverns, gambling casinos. Early July had been converted to winter, indoors. Also, the air-conditioners in private homes could not be shut off. The humblest dwellings, which were normally stifling in the heat of summer, contained less suffering than the mansions of the city.

Parents took their infants to hospitals with severe cases of pneumonia, but the little ones did not recover in the cold there. The weakest and oldest in the nursing homes perished in the frigid night.

Mechanics were unable to stop the functioning of the air conditioners. The temperature in affected buildings continued to drop. Thorne moved his family out into the back yard patio, and they all sought shade during the brightest and hottest parts of the day. They did not go into the house, except to the bathroom.

The monopoly that provided electricity to the city tried to shut off power to the largest buildings, in spite of protests from persons concerned about computer information loss and the humanoid odors of stale air. The machines designed to create cold continued to function, even after the power had been cut off, and the interior temperatures continued to drop.

Families with fireplaces tried to offset the unstoppable cold by building fires in July. The price of firewood soared. Theft of family wood-piles became the focal point of several shooting incidents. The department stores tripled the price of small electric space heaters, and then they became unavailable. The monopoly that provided electricity tripled the rate to users. The governor declared the price increase illegal, and most householders refused to pay. "If they can't shut it off, then that's *their* problem," Thorne announced to his family. An increase in home loss due to fire was noted, caused by attempts to improvise, and burn whatever combustible material could be found. Several cases of asphyxiation, especially of children, were reported, victims of unwise and incorrectly vented contrivances, designed to offset the cold. The price of kitchen matches and book matches, formerly popular with smokers only, suddenly skyrocketed. And then there came a day when there were no matches available at all.

Thorne climbed onto the roof of his home and dismantled the air conditioner, to no avail. With the connecting cable dangling freely in mid-air, the machine continued to hum — the compressor compressed and the fan moved the air. He removed the machine entirely from the roof, and placed it at the curb in front of his house, regarding it as junk to be hauled to the landfill. Machines along the street continued to pump cold air.

The air conditioners continued to chill the space in their vicinity. People no longer made jokes about the cold. More and more of the sick and weak died off. A general malaise settled over the population, a slowing-down, a freezing up, a sense of hopelessness. "Nothing you try works," thought Thorne.

The temperature at the landfill, where all the air conditioning machinery was taken, continued to drop. A snow squall was reported at that end of town, in mid-July. The junked machinery continued to function.

A huge hole was dug by the earth-moving devices employed by the landfill, down to the water table. All the air conditioners were shoved into it and covered over. Life resumed in the city, except that indoor temperatures fluctuated from almost unbearably hot at noon-day to downright chilly at night, that is, the same as outside.

Gardens did not thrive. The leaves on huge deciduous shade

trees turned brown and fell. A drab sort of autumn came at the first of August.

Then individual wells and pumps failed. The city tried to keep it secret, but it was hopeless, as one deep well after another failed. "It's as though the ground water was frozen," one hydrologist admitted.

Fresh holes were drilled, and in every case workers encountered ice at the former water level. "It reminds me of permafrost in Alaska," another worker said.

The site of the burial of the air conditioners at the landfill was reopened. Thorne was part of the group of curious citizen by-standers. The machines were functioning at full throttle. The temperature of the air near them approached absolute zero. "They seem to be sucking energy from the magma," a geologist noted. "Those volcanos weren't plunked there by magic," he added, pointing to the lava plugs which were landmarks on the west side of town. When a by-stander suggested that magma was *hot*, not cold, the geologist retorted, "That's what makes this such an unusual phenomenon. Some kind of heat exchange is going on. Of course, that's what the air-conditioner was originally designed to do, right?"

Tourism has dropped in the area. The only strangers visiting are meteorologists and climatologists, wanting to be present at the inception of a new Ice Age.

◇   ◇   ◇

Toys and Money

Queen Veronica was in a royal pout. "What's the use of being queen, if I can't have what I want?" she asked her governess, interrupting the arithmetic lessons.

Queen Veronica was ten years old, and had been queen for only a short time, since her father, the king, and her mother, the former queen, had been struck and killed by a drunk chariot driver.

Lady Anita, the Governess, was supervising the young queen's education. "And what *do* you want?" Lady Anita asked.

"I want a huge army. I want the army to parade out there in the plaza every day. I want an army so big it takes them all day to march past my balcony. I want to be able to go out there at any time and see the soldiers marching."

"Who says you can't have it?" Lady Anita asked.

"My enemy, the Royal Treasurer!" the queen snarled. "I hate him!"

Lady Anita decided not to ask more, since she wasn't sure who really ran the queendom, with a queen so young and inexperienced.

The queen continued with her list of what she wanted. "I want that huge army to have many changes of uniforms, so they can parade in different colors every day. A yellow army one day, and a blue army the next. Then a red army! Then a green army! Orange, purple, brown, black, white — how many is that?"

"How many colors?" Lady Anita asked.

"Yes. How many?"

"Three, six, seven, eight — *nine* different colors."

"Add grey, and make it ten!" the queen ordered.

"I'm afraid I'm not the one to tend to that," the Governess said. "The Royal Treasurer — "

"Send for him," the queen ordered.

"Yes, Your Royal Highness," Lady Anita said, and curtsied and went out.

The Royal Treasurer listened once again to the demands of Queen Veronica, that a huge army should march through the plaza every day, each day in uniforms of a different color, with ten different dress parade uniform colors rotating every ten days.

"It cannot be done, Your Highness," the Treasurer stated.

The queen shrieked in rage. "That's revolution!"

"No, Your Highness. It is only arithmetic. Ask your governess to teach you two things: One, where soldiers come from, and Two, the meaning of negative numbers. Even queens must obey the laws of arithmetic."

"Who made those laws? I didn't. Am I not the *queen?*"

"You are queen, but you are queen in a world in which the laws of arithmetic must be obeyed."

"I will *not obey them!*" she shouted.

"You will," he answered very quietly. "We all will." The Royal Treasurer turned to the Governess. "I suggest you take up negative numbers immediately."

"She says she hates our work with numbers," the Governess told him.

"I am not surprised," the Royal Treasurer sighed.

Lady Anita went straight to work with the queen's new lessons. She wrote "10" on the royal blackboard. Under it she wrote "100," and then put in the subtraction sign.

"You told me just yesterday," the queen said, "that we can't subtract a big number from a little number. I remember you saying that."

The governess smiled. "You *will* understand negative numbers, I see."

The next day the arithmetic lessons were interrupted by great shouts from the plaza, "Long live the queen!" Queen Veronica ran to the balcony and saw soldiers below, marching in step, marching in rows, all dressed in dull dirty-green colored uniforms. Between shouts of, "Long live the queen!" she could hear the tramp of the feet of the soldiers, marching in time.

The Royal Treasurer appeared beside the queen on the balcony. "Your army is marching, Your Highness. Are you pleased?"

"I am not," the queen stated. "The uniforms are an ugly color."

"It's called drab," he told her.

"It's ugly," she repeated.

The parade lasted all day. The Treasurer insisted that Queen Veronica stay on the balcony and continue to review the troops. At first she was glad to get out of lessons with Lady Anita, but after a while she felt tired of it.

"I'd rather do arithmetic," she complained to the governess.

Lady Anita only smiled, but she did not move away from the balcony.

The queen noticed that the soldiers marching beneath her looked tired. Their marching lines were not as straight as before, and their steps were less lively. Their voices sounded weary, when they called out, "Long live the queen!"

The queen studied the outer edges of the plaza, and then turned to Lady Anita and said, "It's the same group of people marching through here, out that arch, through the back streets the other way and then back into the plaza over there through that other arch." She pointed to the street where soldiers were entering the plaza and heading toward her balcony. "That's stupid!" the queen exclaimed.

"Isn't that what you wanted?" Lady Anita asked.

"I said I wanted a huge army, not an exhausted one." Then she asked her governess, "Where *do* soldiers come from?"

"They come from the families of your queendom. Fathers, brothers, sons, daughters — and they come from all the places where people work — farms, bakeries, clothing factories, shoe factories, paper mills, steel mills."

"So, a small army is plenty. If everybody is marching, who

will do the work?" said the queen, after thinking about it.

"And who will pay all the soldiers?" Lady Anita asked.

"Pay them? Does somebody *pay* them? Who?" the queen asked.

"The queendom pays them," the governess explained. "That's why you're learning about negative numbers. If you have soldiers instead of workers, you're trying to subtract a big number from a little number."

"That's stupid," the queen said.

"So I've heard," said the governess.

The queen thought some more. She seemed to grow up a little. She wondered how to change her list of what she wanted. Twice recently she called it stupid. But she *did* love parades.

"A parade every day, all day every day, really is too much," she finally said to Lady Anita. "The Treasurer is right — people have work to do. We don't need an army, just because I like parades."

Just then the Royal Treasurer joined them on the balcony. "Let's have a parade on special holidays, and a big one on my birthday," the queen continued, "but the people can parade in their special work clothes — farmers, bakers, spinners, weavers, cobblers. Yes! That'll be even more fun!"

The Royal Treasurer bowed low in front of Queen Veronica. "Yes, Your Highness. It shall be done."

◇   ◇   ◇

Night Light

A weary man, lost at night, sees a light. A tiny light, far off. Far, far away. He is encouraged and travels toward it. The night is very dark. He sees no stars, no sky, no landscape in front of him. He reaches down to touch the ground and finds it cold and bare of grass or any growing thing. He sees the light far off, and wonders if he could have stumbled into a cave somehow. He remembers a phrase from long ago — "the light at the end of the tunnel," and a scene from a novel of even longer ago, of a boy and girl lost in a cave after their last candle has burned out.

He moves toward the tiny light ahead of him and feels that he is not inside, but outside.

Suddenly he is surrounded by many lights, in a field of knee-high grass. He is delighted, and regards the thousands of fireflies that surround him as company. He feels less lost, less alone in a barren world. The fireflies ignore him, flying and blinking. The man chuckles when it occurs to him that they are totally unaware of his presence and are only interested in each other. They mean much to him, as fellow live creatures, but he means nothing to them.

We used to call them lightning bugs, as kids, he thinks. He had never seen so many in one place. The field and the world glow with a steady light, even though each individual source of light blinks on and off with a regular rhythm. He lies down in the field and falls asleep.

When he awakens it is completely dark again. He can see nothing before him, not even his own hand before his face. He recalls how that childhood phrase used to refer to "really dark." He can see nothing in the sky, and can see no sky at all. "Dark, all dark!" The music from Handel's *Samson* passes through his head, along with the thought, "Maybe I'm blind."

Then he sees the tiny light again. It seems to be far off. He heads toward it. He is not walking on grass.

He loses the light after a while and stops. Then he finds it again, behind him. He turns around and heads toward it.

Again he loses it, and finds it behind him. He wonders if it is moving, but when he stands still for a long time and studies it, it remains in the same place. He is the only thing moving.

He goes toward it, and loses it again. I keep going past it, he decides to himself. He finds it and moves very slowly and very deliberately toward it.

He finds that he is much bigger than the light. He feels huge. The light is tiny. It is nearby, very close, but tiny. He stops, kneels down finally, in order to study it.

He peers in through a tiny window, into a tiny room. He sees a fireplace, some stools, a table, a tiny woman nursing a tiny baby, singing to the baby.

He cannot get into that room. He is too big, vastly too big. And he cannot make his presence known to the woman — it is too dark. She would be afraid. He feels afraid.

What has happened to my world? he wonders. What has happened to me? Where is everybody? Must we do this, too, alone?

For a brief moment he is tempted to smash the tiny room, light and inhabitants and all, but he does not. The stories of ogres and evil giants go through his mind. So, I am one of them, after all, he thinks. He sits down to watch the tender scene beside the tiny fire inside the tiny room. I wouldn't want to hurt them, or anybody, he thinks.

He sits down to watch, to sleep. He dreams that the dark world he is wandering on is an atom in an ugly scar on the hind leg of a crippled lightning bug.

◇   ◇   ◇

Something in the Cellar

Missy and her father sat at the kitchen table, eating breakfast. "Daddy, you've really gotta get that cellar pumped out. There's two feet of water down there. That old stove of Grandma's is ruined. Who knows what all else."

"No hurry, then, if everything's ruined," her father said. Missy didn't understand her father very well. He wasn't exactly lazy. He went to work every day. But he let things go.

"Couldn't it hurt the foundation of the house, or something?" she asked. "When there's a flood downtown, people have their cellars pumped out right away."

"Let me worry about it, will you?" he growled.

"Besides," Missy went on, more serious, "I think there's something living down there. Something's in the cellar, Daddy!"

"Don't be silly."

"No, I hear it."

"It's just the water."

"Something's *in* the water. I can hear something sloshing around sometimes, making noises like you make in the bathtub."

"Not me."

"Sometimes I hear something dripping. And I come and open the cellarway door and listen, and I can hear something moving in the water."

"No, you can't."

"I can," she insisted. "It's like when I'm swimming at the creek, and trying to swim across without making a sound, and an arm or a leg comes up too close to the surface, and there's a sound. *That* sound. I hear that sound in the cellar."

"Maybe it's your grandma," he said, with a grin. It was a strange unpleasant grin that Missy didn't like.

"No," Missy said. "She's gone. You know that."

"She used to live down there, you know," he said, still grinning that mean-looking grin. Then he began to sing:

"Grandma's in the cellar —
Lordy, can't you smell 'er?
Bakin' biscuits on her derned old dirty stove..."

"It's *not* Grandma, Daddy, and you know it! It's not funny!"

"In her eye there is some matter
That keep drippin' in the batter,
And she whistles while the stuff runs down her nose."

Her father laughed

"That's a disgusting song!" Missy exclaimed.

"I know," he grinned. "It's hilarious."

"You still need to pump out that water. Something's in the cellar!"

◇ ◇ ◇

Biscuits. Blank. Flavor.

Grandma. Taste. Sharp. Mean. Meanness. Food. LongTime. Water. Keep.

Water. Sound. TimeLong. Hatch. Bottom. Plug. HoleWall. Tunnel. Water.

Alone. No. Frogs. Mice. Rats. Muskrat. Water. Grandma. Goodtaste. Meanness. PlentyMeat.

Noises. Thump. Scrape. Yell. MachineTalk. Above.

Water. Sound. Quiet. LoudSplash. Catch. Eat. Sleep. Below.

◇ ◇ ◇

Some days later Missy and her father were again talking at the kitchen table.

"Why doesn't Mama call or write?" Missy asked.

"How should I know?" her father answered. "Maybe she's avoiding you."

"She's staying away from *you*, more likely. Does she write to you?"

"No."

"Why doesn't she write to me?"

"I have no idea."

"Where is she?"

"I don't know that either."

"It's been months."

"Has it?"

"And when are you going to pump out that water? There's something in the cellar!"

◇ ◇ ◇

Missy. Mother. Abandon. No. Father. BringBack. Feed. Mother. FlavorGood. Meanness. Plenty. Grandma. More.

◇ ◇ ◇

Missy's father called the TV repairman. Missy was not at home. The man came and repaired the TV set. Then the two men disagreed about the bill. They argued. They yelled and scuffled. Missy's father struck the TV repairman on the head with a frying pan, knocking him unconscious. He threw the man down the cellar stair. The man's neck was broken and he drowned in the water.

Missy's father heard a sudden rush of water, rapid violent movement in the water in the cellar. He knew perfectly well that there was something in the cellar.

◇ ◇ ◇

Food. Good. ChangeFlavor. Mean. MeannessNew. Petty. Cheater. Hater. No. LifetimeHate. No. Small. Mean. Good.
Mother. Different. Mean. LifePurpose. Mean. Habit. Mean. Heart. Mean.
Grandma. Different. Meanness. LargeLarge. Strong.
Father. Meanness. LargeLargeLarge. Hate. GuiltHate. Flavor. DreamFeast. Later. Someday.

◇ ◇ ◇

Missy began to worry about strange smells that were coming up from the cellar. She told her father, but he just laughed at her. "You're imagining things," he said.

"No," she exclaimed. "Something's in the cellar. Something's rotting in the cellar."

"Forget it," he growled.

"I won't."

She called the Public Health Department and two men came from the office downtown. They arrived just before her father came home from work. Her father admitted to them that he needed to have the cellar pumped out. "I've been very busy," he told the officials.

"Something's living down there," Missy told them.

"Some what thing?" one man asked.

"I don't know. Something. It lives in the water," Missy said.

"She has a very vivid imagination," her father told them.

"Let's have a look," the other official said.

"Oh, that's not necessary," her father said. "I'll just have it pumped."

An official opened the cellarway door, and the men went down several steps and then stopped. They shone their flashlights on the partly submerged stove, and on the surface of the water. Nothing moved, but they went down no further.

"This is not sanitary, Sir," one official said.

"And it's not safe," stated the other. "This could undermine the foundation of your house."

"I know. I'll tend to it," Missy's father growled.

The men left.

Missy could see that her father was furious. He swung a fist at her, but she ducked and avoided the worst of the punch, which glanced off the top of her head. He swung again and she ran. He chased her across the kitchen. She ran into the cellarway to hide from him, and he slammed the door behind her. She screamed in the pitch dark and fell to the floor, pounding on the door.

She heard her father laugh. She screamed again, "Daddy! Let me out!"

He laughed again and she heard him tramp across the kitchen, across the living room, and out the front door.

She was alone. It was dark. It smelled a little strange, that same rotting smell that made her call the public health people.

Missy's terror subsided a little as time passed and nothing happened. Her eyes grew accustomed to the dark. She sat on the top step and stared down into the cellar. She heard the water sound, like someone moving in a huge bathtub.

◇   ◇   ◇

Fear. Flavor. New. MeannessNone. Food. TasteNone. DesireNone. Show. Shape. Missy. FearNone. Friends. Maybe. Food. MeannessGood. GoodnessNo. Friend. NeedFriend.

◇   ◇   ◇

Missy went up into the rest of the house, when her father was gone to work. She ate fruit and bread and peanut butter. She drank water. She went to the bathroom. She took a bath.

She brought down an old sleeping bag. She made stepping stones out of old washtubs placed up-side-down, and an old table. When her father was at home — evenings, all night, early mornings — she stayed on a wide, dry shelf near the ceiling of the cellar, dry and warm.

She made friends with whatever it was that lived in the cellar with her. She called it her monster. She was puzzled as to what it was. Sometimes it had very little shape, when it seemed to be sleeping. When she stared at it, that seemed to awaken it, and it coiled and uncoiled and raised a face, a really very friendly face, and looked at her.

When the TV was on upstairs, she talked to it very softly. "Hello. My name is Missy. Can we be friends?" It never spoke words, but seemed to understand, like a dog, or a parrot, perhaps. But when they stared into each other's faces, with both sets of eyes accustomed to what wasn't as dark as seemed at first, she felt she could hear words, deep inside her head. "Friends. Yes. Meanness. No. Fear. No."

Missy became a missing person. From her shelf she could hear her father's conversation with the police. "She's gone to live with her mother."

"The school should have been notified."

"I'll tend to it. Watery smell? I need to have the cellar pumped out."

After the police left, Missy called softly, "Daddy!" Very softly. "Daddy, come down." She heard his footsteps stop, above her, and was sure he heard her.

◇   ◇   ◇

Missy. Friend. FearNone. MeannessNone.

◇   ◇   ◇

Missy's father brought a date home one evening. The date heard Missy calling, "Daddy! Come on down."

"You don't hear it?" the woman asked him.

"No. You're imagining things."

"Let's go downstairs, and check."

"No."

"Something's in the cellar."

"You're crazy," he said.

Missy heard the date walk to the cellarway door, open it, step to the first stair, and stop.

The woman stayed a long time. Missy didn't move, and neither did whatever else was living in the cellar. The door closed. Missy heard the woman say, "That's disgusting. You should tend to it."

◇   ◇   ◇

Friends. Play. Fetch. Bones. Missy. Like.

◇   ◇   ◇

Missy regarded the water creature as her friend. The two of them did something very strange. The creature brought her head bones from under water. She lined them up in a row on Grandma's dirty old stove. Then she sang the song:

"Grandma's in the cellar —
Lordy, can't you smell 'er?
Bakin' biscuits on her derned old dirty stove...
In her eye there is some matter
That keep drippin' in the batter,
And she whistles while the stuff runs down her nose."

She talked without spoken words to the creature. Sometimes they talked a little past each other. They agreed that they wanted her father to come down into the cellar.

Missy used to turn on the water in the old wash tubs, when her father was upstairs watching TV. It made the pipes groan. The noise roused him. They could hear him pacing the floor. The creature made its watery sloshing noises. Missy called up, very softly, cooing, "Daddy! Come on down."

Her father came to the cellarway door and opened it. Missy and her friend were absolutely quiet. He closed the door and went to the living room. She called again. They could hear him throwing things up there.

Missy called again, "Daddy! Come down."

He jerked the cellarway door open and shone a flashlight down. In the beam of light, Missy was displayed sitting on Grandma's derned old dirty stove, behind a row of grisly, grinning skulls.

Her father came down the stairs. "What the hell are you doing? Get over here."

"You come get me, Daddy," Missy called softly.

The man stepped into the water, in over his knees. "It's disgusting," he began, but a huge swishing watery wave-sound startled him. He stumbled and fell headlong face down into the water.

◇   ◇   ◇

Flavor. Strong. Meanness. GoodGood. Plenty.
Missy. Friend. CryCry. Goodbye.

◇   ◇   ◇

Fertility Problems

Well, here we are at mid-century. We're still here, even though many prophets of doom, at the turn of the millennium, predicted that we would not be. Humanity is more resilient, and more ingenious, than those who claimed to foresee the end were able to imagine.

Actually, the doom-saying began two centuries earlier, when Thomas Malthus calculated impending disaster, based on the difference between addition and multiplication. The food supply increases by addition, while the human population increases by multiplication. The difference between 1,2,3,4,5 and 2,4,8,16,32 is remarkable, and three more steps make it even more startling — 6,7,8 compared to 64,128,256.

Malthus, and other experts in arithmetic, predicted disaster for humanity. But it didn't happen. Our numbers increased by multiplication, without doubt, from six billion to fifteen billion in our lifetime, but we averted disaster by consuming the earth and the Biosphere at an even greater rate. We were converting the Biosphere itself into humanity. Cassandras and Jeremiahs continued to say that we couldn't do that, but we did continue to do it.

Zoologists noticed, more than a century ago, that when a species experiences overcrowding, the females tend to become infertile. It was noted in foxes, and coyotes, before they became extinct early in this century. It has been noticed in rats, which are by no means extinct.

Ancient myths referred to infertile female humans as "barren." It was a slur, implying that the barren individual had failed to accomplish her principal function in life. Stories of how this curse of barrenness was overcome elevated the successful ones to places of very high esteem, as in the cases of Sarah, Rachel, Hannah and Elizabeth.

When some individual women, in the last century, banded together to repudiate the notion that reproduction was the principle, if not exclusive, function for women, they encountered severe opposition. In the name of individual liberty the women insisted that they could live full rich human lives without giving birth, even without having husbands. All the weight of the ancient mythology of patriarchy was pressed against them.

As overcrowding became an obvious factor, as seen in the steadily declining individual standard of living, "barren" women were held up as heroines, willing to forego what had long been held as the very purpose of a female human life, for the long-term good of the species. Meanwhile the myth people raged, and called these outspoken women "witches, bitches and Nazis."

Nature seemed to be influencing the human fertility rate somewhat, as with coyotes and rats. More and more couples came to the medical establishment seeking help with problems of infertility. Human ingenuity rose to the occasion with new techniques: artificial insemination, sperm and egg banks, *in vitro* fertilization, and implantation in surrogate mothers. Infertility was virtually overcome, even though ensuing legal questions became rampant, serious, and until recently insoluble.

Nature seemed to be participating in another way. Homosexuality has existed among humans for several millennia, if not forever, but the inclination and the practice became much more widespread before the turn of the century. Individuals "came out," and banded together seeking political expression and "clout," and arousing remarkably virulent opposition.

Since homosexuals are, by definition infertile, as long as they practice homosexuality exclusively, some scholars hypothesized that this burgeoning "life-style," as it was called, was Nature responding to overcrowding again, by making individuals, in effect, infertile.

An epidemic raged among male homosexuals in the decades before the turn of the century, which the adherents of ancient patriarchal myth labeled divine punishment on the life-style they disapproved of. But when the epidemic spread and grew among heterosexuals, the research became serious, the source of the new virus at the biochemical warfare laboratories was exposed, and the antidote revealed. Nature fights overcrowding by means of pestilence, as well as infertility, but in this case "nature" used the human passion for war, and disaster was only narrowly averted.

Meanwhile human ingenuity was at work to overcome the infertility of homosexuals. Artificial insemination was commonly used, enabling female couples to bear and rear children. The ongoing increase of human population was left almost unaffected.

Then, just before the turn to this first century of the third millennium, scientists and scholars began to notice something new. The year was 1996, to be exact. Several different studies, with different bottom-line figures, but identical implications for humanity's future, were reported. One, from Scotland, showed that the sperm count in human males dropped by 24%, comparing males born in 1958 with those born in 1970. Another study, from France, found that the sperm counts of donors at a Paris sperm bank had dropped by one-third over the previous two decades. Another study, from Denmark, showed that the sperm count in general had dropped by 50% over the previous fifty years.

No alarm was raised over these studies. Only one spermatozoan is required to fertilize an egg, and the lowered sperm count still left thousands to do the task. When the scholars tried to hypothesize about the causes of the lowered sperm count, they had little data. Science at the turn of the century had little interest in causes and prevention, preferring to concentrate on "cures," which could generate huge profits for the corporations funding the research.

Air pollution in general, estrogen, plastic bags — all were suggested, unconvincingly, as possible causes. Radiation, a known cause of infertility in all mammals, was not put forth as a cause. Too much profit was generated in all those enterprises, and therefore the "scholarship" was easily dismissed as "inconclusive."

But humanity survived the great Die-off of the 2020's and 2030's — and here we are, still alive and kicking. When the next crop of clones is decanted, just after we enter the second half of the 21st century, the population of the world will double. And we'll continue to multiply. There is a certain justifiable satisfaction to be felt in proving that the prophets of doom have been wrong once again.

◊ ◊ ◊

High Tech

I'm reading away, trying to stay informed about what's going on in the world, and I throw *THE NATION* down, not in disgust with the editors and writers of that weekly paper, but in desperation. I mean, one can only stand so much truth at a time, when the news is as bad as all that. I need comic relief, and I don't mean *THE PROGRESSIVE* or *IN THESE TIMES*.

So I start through the junk mail and come to a blurb, offering me a summary of the most up-to-date information I can possibly have any use for, in a new magazine called, *HIGH TECHNOLOGY*. I begin reading and before long I'm close to panic. I mean, if we don't blow the world to smithereens, the computers are going to take over everything! What a choice! I stare at the brochure, and things begin to go into motion. I'm looking at the pictures and reading the captious little descriptions, and pretty soon I'm hearing voices.

"The computers are making an artificial world, which will have artificial people in it."

(The question is, 'Can the computers rescue the world from the mere humans in time, before they really do blow it all away or poison it irremediably?')

"The artificial man which the computers are creating already has, or is, the following: a demineralized bone jaw, artificial blood, dacron blood vessels, collagen implanted teeth, artificial skin, artificial muscle tissue, an artificial liver, an artificial pancreas, dacron tendons, an Insall/Burstein posterior stabilized knee, an artificial kidney, a prosthetic arm, artificial lungs, and a Jarvic heart. He will live longer and suffer less pain."

(But who will he be?)

"Guided wave optics will make the telephone system into an

integrated digital network, which will be at the same time the world's largest computer. This will become the brain of the new post-human culture/creature. Micro-computers and cordless phones will enable the computer to keep all individual humans plugged in at all times."

This is the so-called "information super-highway," just a few moments in the future. I'm interested, but I'm fearful of becoming just a piece of someone else's information.

(Leave that cordless phone on the table and walk out of the house, and spend a day at the park! You forget what it feels like.)

I am becoming all those artificial parts. The older part of me may forget who I really am.

(That's the part to hang on to! Stay awake!)

I am awake, but I'm still hearing voices.

"The video games keep a person occupied, for long stretches at a time. From computerized information sources, he learns more than he wants or needs to know. He never thinks about things much — he's always interfacing and being fed *more* information."

(See! That's enough! Take just that much in and digest it. Let the rest go by. You're drowning yourself in information. You need to put what information you already have to work.)

It passes through my mind that the solar heater salesman is against nuclear.

(What?!)

He said so this afternoon while selling me a solar hot-air collector. We also talked about plutonium and leukemia and half-life. We compared the age of human civilization to 250,000 years, and became alarmed.

(Are you processing information correctly?)

The machine checks you when you're sick. That lady in the brochure is having her lovely breasts examined by machine. A nurse is holding the machine, perhaps reading a dial on it. The doctor will type what that nurse reads into another computer.

(The doctor and the nurse constitute a two-link human chain, only, inside the computer!)

"Medicines will consist of monoclonal antibodies, which do to you what they've been programmed to do. 'Remove Virus-X —' and, zap! Virus-X is gone."

Who programs these things? Who's in charge here?

"Wars will be fought by superfighters equipped with digital maps and sophisticated navigational systems including a signal that puts the image of the airplane itself on its own map — this machine is already a little turned in on itself."

Yes, the last war, which wasn't exactly a war at all, since "the enemy" never fired back, is now troubling people because the casualties were caused by our own men and our own computers, what they so cleverly call, "friendly fire."

And I'm perfectly aware that it's because of the computers and the simulated war games that the hawks want a war every once in a while — so they can test it all, play with it, put it to work, justify its existence. They waste all that money making their toys, and risk all our lives testing it, and kill a lot of innocent people at both ends of that process — and it should be stopped.

(Well, stop it, then! You humans still have time. Don't let them take over.)

Who? The computers?

(No, the hawks! What they're doing could stop the whole process, and deprive us computers of our chance to take over, and save, the world.)

"The computer will go from drafting and number crunching to Computer Aided Design and join with Computer Aided Manufacturing to create a system in which the computers will be committing reproduction, taking the new product's development all the way from conception to the end of the production line."

(See! Give us a chance!)

Who, the computers? Say, who are you anyway? You inside the parentheses, there? Are you man, or computer?

(I'll never tell. But you really do need to get those maniacs stopped. They're a menace to all of us.)

Well, you're right. *THE NATION* says that, too.

"This is essentially a magazine for businessmen. In regular features you get fast-reading coverage of technology's impact on the factory, the office, medicine, military and aerospace efforts, consumers, the stock market, social and economic affairs. The 'Business Outlook' section adds solid financial facts to the technological excitement, and helps you focus on what's most significant from an economic point of view."

(Let me note that you business people will be blown away, too, if those guys aren't stopped.)

You think so?

(They're totally irrational. Hawks don't think clearly. They believe their own falsehoods. We suggest that the business community withdraw support from them now, even at the cost of some fat contracts. It is time for weaning. Just inform them that you don't want to make that stuff anymore, that you have enough. In fact, you have too much already.)

Yes. Makes sense. I wonder if we could use all this high tech to clean up the mess they've already made?

(Certainly, you could. But you have to decide that that's what you're going to do with technology.)

Let's try it. Hey, you high tech folks! Look at this mess! Nuclear waste here. Chemical waste there. My God, it's to the point now that the old anglo-saxon word for organic waste refers to a scarce and friendly substance. We need more of it, not less! We need to get this chemical/nuclear non-crap out of here. Hey, you! You computers! Get this nuclear non-crap out of here!

(Yassuh, Boss. Right away, Boss.)

And you hawks! Cool it. You'll just have to re-tool, after all. So begin now. Before you make any more mess.

◇   ◇   ◇

My daydream, which ended rather pleasantly, was interrupted by a visit from my chronically depressed buddy, Clarence. His first words, after flopping into the easy chair in my office, were, "The computers have become smarter than the humans."

"No, Clarence," I said. "It just seems that way. Smart humans can use them to help lord it over dull-witted ones, but the computer is just a machine."

"Accounts Payable says I have to wait another month, because the computer was down last week, that it only writes checks on the twenty-fourth, unless it's a Wednesday, or full moon." Clarence was so down, I almost missed his sarcasm.

"I have a computer, Clarence. It works fine. It works at any time of the day or night, any day of the month, any month. All I have to do is turn it on, and it does what I tell it. Full moon has no effect on it. Not even the current bank balance has any effect on it."

My sad friend shook his head. "There is real danger that the computers will wrest power from the humans, absolutely."

"No, Clarence. As I say, some humans use the computer to wield power over others."

"The computers have completely ruined my life," he groaned.

"How so?"

"The phone company says I owe them a hundred and fifty thousand dollars."

"It's obviously an error."

"Yes, but there's no correcting it."

"Who could possibly owe the phone company that much?"

"The guy who tormented that fundamentalist preacher, by calling his 800 number automatically day and night for three months."

"But that wasn't you," I said.

"The phone company's computer thinks so."

"But it's an error."

"I know. But it can't be corrected."

"Sure, it can."

"They insist that I must pay it. They're suing me already. They have liens on my house and car, my son's farm — everything."

"What's your son have to do with it?"

"He refused to add 'Junior' to his name, uses the same name, and they've grabbed everything."

"I'm sure it can be cleared up. If not, you may have to declare bankruptcy, to save your home." I felt sad, at such a suggestion. Clarence's retort was almost triumphant. "I can't declare bankruptcy."

"Why not?"

"The computer at the bank says I have a balance of seven hundred thousand. The court is assuming that that's correct. I thought I had seven hundred."

"Well, it's all a mistake."

"I assume so. But when I tried to get them to pay the hundred and fifty thousand, and let me settle for the rest, the girl at the bank just smiled."

"She did? What did she say?"

"Computer error!"

Rituals

"If we add any more rituals to our lives, there won't be any life left — it'll be all ritual!" That exclamation from my wife caused me to stop, and think, and then begin making notes. I was frankly quite startled by the volume of time and effort we spend on what she called rituals.

What caught her attention was what could be called "body maintenance."

[1] Brush your teeth, after flossing thoroughly every single tooth. It is best to do this after every meal. I do it every evening before going to bed, and also at other times, usually before going out to be with other people.

[2] Take a bath. I do this daily, if not after getting sweaty gardening or shoveling compost, or before going out for the evening, then before going to bed.

[3] Shave. My wife is excused from this one, as are two of our four sons, who allow full beards to grow. Trim your moustache and sideburns. I do the shaving before every bath, and the trimming when the need has become obvious.

[4] Wash your hands and face and comb your hair. I do this upon arising in the morning. I wash my hands, with strong hand soap, several times a day, depending on what I'm doing.

[5] Wash your hair. I do this every third or fourth day in winter, every other day in summer. Since we don't have a shower, it takes considerable effort and bodily contortion to get the job done in our small bathtub.

[6] Arrange for your wife to trim your hair, about once a month. Startle a barber about twice a year. I let it be longer in winter than in summer. My wife has her hair done by a beautician about three times a month.

[7] Trim your fingernails. It seems to me that I need to do this very often, and oftener than formerly. If I don't trim them with the clippers that were invented and designed precisely for that task, they split or break and I'm tempted to trim them with my teeth, and never stop the process until I'm down to the quick.

[8] Trim your toenails. If I don't, they tear holes in my socks. The trimming is harder to do at this stage of life. I'm less supple, and what needs trimming has taken on the thickness and consistency of horn.

[9] Eat three meals a day, at consistent times. Sit down together and visit with each other. It needs to be a shared ritual, we believe. We do this, not as formally as those families with servants depicted in movies and TV shows, but much more formally than those who simply grab and run. Mealtime for us is a ritual we know we need.

[10] Take your pills. I am not on any medication. With breakfast I take one multiple-vitamin pill, 1000 mg of vitamin C and 250 mg of calcium.

[11] Have a daily bowel movement, complete with careful washing and anointing afterwards. If this isn't a daily occurrence, at nearly the same time of day every day, then it isn't a ritual — it's a problem. We regard this "regularity" as one of the surest signs of our good health.

[12] Do some kind of body work. Some walk, some jog, some run, some go to the gym and work out, some have different kinds of exercise machinery in the home. We do T'ai Ch'ih Chih, every morning before breakfast together. It is a fifteen-minute shared ritual. The movements "stir the energy, and balance the energy." We believe it helps regulate appetite, weight and elimination. For me it releases endorphins, which amount to a natural mood elevator and regulator. If I wasn't ready for a new day before T'ai Ch'ih, I'm transformed and ready for anything, when we finish.

[13] Get a consistent amount of sleep, going to bed and rising at regular times every night. We do this. My wife needs more

time at sleep than I. I stay up one hour later than she does, reading. We rise at the same time, with no alarm clock. I am awakened by daylight, later in winter than in summer. The tinkering with the labelling of the hours by Daylight Savings is mildly troublesome to us. It takes us about a week, every fall and every spring, to readjust.

[14] Get into position for sleep. I need to place my arms very consciously, one on my hip, the other crooked under the pillow, lying on my left side. If I don't, I wake up pushing my fist into the mattress, my shoulder in pain, my wrist "asleep," because of a pinched nerve. I presume this is a ritual not everyone has to bother with, but by learning to do it, I have gone back to sleeping all night, after not doing so for years.

[15] Tend to your neck. A chiropractor has lost hundreds in fees, by sharing with me a "trick." Lie still, flat on your back, in the position the yogis call "soaking up the prana," with a towel rolled tightly into a roll as thick as your arm and placed under your neck. It prevents neck stiffness, and straightens the back without violence. I do this for five to ten minutes, after waking and before rising in the morning.

◇   ◇   ◇

Rituals. Preventive maintenance for the body. But noting it all down does make it seem like a very great deal of activity. No wonder my wife feared that rituals would take up the whole of life. And yet there is more, much more.

There are preventive maintenance rituals for the house which include washing dishes, vacuuming the floor, bringing in fire wood, building fires, removing ashes, disposing of junk mail. There are similar rituals for the car, for the rototiller, for the computer. There are financial rituals, including paying the bills and balancing the check-book. There is that daily ritual in which we look for surprises — going to the mailbox and the post office box. Sometimes it isn't all junk.

There are rituals that we must go through every time we leave the house. Check the fireplace. Check the thermostat and the fans. Check the doors and windows. Arm correctly the burglar alarm.

Meal preparation can be a ritual. Our breakfast especially has become that, since we eat the same things every morning. We have found what we really like and what seems to do us the most good. We include half a cup of Kombucha tea — and I have the weekly ritual of the preparation of the tea, which has taken on a ceremonial character, somewhat like the Japanese tea ceremony, even though I'm alone when I do it. I go through the same motions in the same order each time, and find a comfort in the repetition, and in the results.

Besides the bodily, physical rituals, there are rituals of the mind. Some use missals, prayer books, lectionaries and the Bible. We have a broader reach. We both love reading and do it every day. A day without it feels incomplete.

Meditation is very important. We have not made it into a rigid routine, as many recommend, and we don't do it, as yogis do, for hours at a time. Some of them do it virtually all the time. Some would give these serious meditators credit for helping to keep the universe on course, for helping to hold the world together. There is a state of heightened awareness, which meditation has to do with, and we are, without deliberate self-conscious effort, trying to be in that state more and more.

We have both become part of that modern movement, in which writing is the new meditation. Scribbling in spiral notebooks, absolutely private notebooks, unless the author is reading aloud, which we do sometimes. That kind of writing is a form of meditation, in which we come into contact with the subconscious awareness that lies beneath all things. Keep the hand moving. Grammar and vocabulary are less important that the flow itself. What is produced, especially at first, is less important than the sometimes startling sense of fresh awareness that comes.

Rituals keep the two of us bonded to each other. Doing T'ai Ch'ih together is very important. Eating together, and sharing food with others together, is a basic part of our lives. Talking together — telling the other simply what happened to each one out there in the world while we were separated, sharing the reading, laughing, smiling, noting the ironies of life and the grim droll humor of aging gracefully — these have become almost rituals by now. She is right. Life is become all ritual. But it's not a bad thing, not at all.

◊　◊　◊

The Chinese Plan

Grandpa was upset. "I can see why they think they have to do it, but it's going to change things that we thought were *basic!*"

"Who? What?" I asked. I can be in the same room with the TV on and not hear a thing. Grandpa wonders how I do it. He was watching the news.

"The Chinese. They're insisting now that families have only *one* child!" He shut the TV off. "They have to get their population growth under control — I understand that. My God, there are a *billion* of 'em! But it's gonna be strange."

"Can they do it? Make families have only one child?"

"I don't know. They look serious about it to me. They're good at putting social pressure on individuals. And they don't have any religious leaders to interfere."

"So what's bothering you about it?"

"One child per family — they'll do away with words like 'brother' and 'sister.' They'll really change things, basic things."

"I guess that's right," I said. I don't have any brothers or sisters. Mom's in Europe, and she doesn't intend to have any more kids. I heard her say that to her new husband. I don't think she intended for me to hear it, but I did.

Grandpa burst out again. "My God, in another generation they'll do away with words like 'aunt' and 'uncle' — and 'cousin!' There won't be any such things. Or they'll be illegal, maybe criminal, if they really pull this off."

I wasn't as upset as Grandpa. I don't have any aunts or uncles or cousins, either, that we know about. Mom was Grandpa's only child, and we never found out anything about my Dad's family. "You don't like to see words die out, is that it?" I asked.

59

"It's not just the words. It's a lot of things that we've taken for granted for ever." He had a lot of brothers and sisters, but he's not in touch with them much, that I know of. Some are dead, and he's on the outs with the rest. He calls himself "the black sheep." Funny phrase. They think he's a little crazy, and for that matter, so do the neighbors around here. I don't. He's just more logical than most folks, and more thoughtful, maybe.

◇ ◇ ◇

We watched another program on the Chinese plan, on educational TV. Grandpa was pleased that I was interested. I remembered his worry about the words, 'brother,' 'sister,' 'aunt,' 'uncle,' and 'cousin,' and got to thinking afterward.

"Grandpa, the Chinese plan may work better than ours."

"How so? We should limit our families to two, I think, just because of *world* over-population, but there'd still be brothers and sisters and cousins, if we did that. And there's no such plan, anyway."

"I was thinking about something else. People say, 'Brotherhood will be the solution to the problems of discrimination and oppression and war.' I've heard you say that."

"What're you getting at?" he asked.

"See if this makes sense. In China both mother and father work full time, right?"

"Right."

"The only kid they're allowed to have will spend most of his time in a public nursery, run by the community."

"Right, again."

"Maybe the Chinese will teach the kids to use the words 'brother' and 'sister' for the other kids in the nursery."

"Maybe."

"And the kids could call the parents of the other kids in the nursery 'aunt' and 'uncle.'"

I saw a light go on, just behind Grandpa's eyes. "Hey! Yeah! Maybe —"

"They could use the word, 'cousin,' for kids raised in *other* nurseries — anywhere."

"Yes! It could be a breakthrough!" Grandpa was excited. "The concept of family, the extended family, would not be lost, not necessarily. Just changed, and enlarged."

I kept going. "'Brother' used to mean, 'Boy who has the same parents I have.' But not any more. There'll be no such thing. I never had one, myself. Now it'll mean, 'Boy in the same nursery.'"

"I like it, I like it," said Grandpa, with a grin.

"'Cousin' will mean, 'Boy or girl approximately my age,'" I continued.

"And we could save the words, 'schoolmate' or 'classmate,' for later, in high school or college —"

"And brotherhood —" I began, and then I stopped.

"It's an old unreachable goal, easy to make fun of, hard to live up to —" Grandpa faltered, too.

"I never had a brother," I repeated. "Do brothers love each other, Grandpa?"

He became very thoughtful. "Not always. It's certainly not automatic. Sometimes they hate each other. Old myths remind us — Cain and Abel, Jacob and Esau. The Chinese have their own myths that say the same thing."

"But maybe, if little kids see other little kids, not as competition — rivals for food and toys and love —" I was losing my train of thought. I wondered if maybe the changing of the word 'brother' could help bring the dream of brotherhood a little closer. I think Grandpa felt that, too, for a little while there. But now we're both stuck again, not sure.

The problem isn't in the words, exactly. I wonder what it is. I don't need a brother, I don't think. But I need friends, or a friend. I guess that's what stays the same.

"The Chinese plan doesn't change the notion of 'grandfather,' does it, Grandpa?"

"Nope," he said, and opened his arms for a hug. I gave him a good one.

◇　◇　◇

Watch on Big River

Robert received an unexpected inheritance when an older friend died, and he went out and spent it on a dream he had nurtured in his mind for a long time. He bought his own radio station. He named it KWBR, and never indicated that the last three letters meant anything.

He was more interested in locally produced music of all sorts than in national trends and hits and stars. He provided an outlet for locally written and produced radio plays. He dedicated a great deal of air time to local news. He sought and aired school news, excluding athletic events and stars, which he felt were already adequately covered. School dramas, school orchestras and jazz combos and mariachi bands, and school art shows all received air time.

Robert was interested in news of locally owned businesses and new business ventures, not national franchises but local and native enterprises. He interviewed local artists and local writers, and publicized shows and readings.

The new station depended on volunteers as DJ's and interviewers. The local artists and writers and musicians did much of the volunteering.

Robert allowed the marketing department to grow on its own. He did not pound the pavement or the telephone wires begging businesses to buy advertising. They came to him, actually pressed their money on him in spite of his reluctance, as the local audience grew.

KWBR launched a new program, which Robert named, "Watch on Big River." A radio station doesn't need a logo quite the way a TV station or a newspaper or a newsletter does, but one came to mind — a lookout atop a rock-tower, shielding his eyes and staring across the river valley to the mesa and the mountains on the other side.

The new program divided itself into a series of what Robert called "chapters." First came the Water Watch chapter. The Big River carried a small amount downstream, compared to the size of the aquifer under the city. How much water is there? Robert brought in hydrology experts, who assured the audience that the supply was not "infinite," as had been said and evidently believed a few short decades earlier. The supply was limited, and was being mined at an alarming rate. The water table had dropped ten to twenty feet in the memory of many listeners. Mythological quantities of the water had been given away to favored industries. Ground water had been contaminated by oil depots, filling stations, military dumps and hospitals. Golf courses consumed a huge percentage of current use. KWBR reported on the flow of water in ways formerly not used by local radio stations. "Radioactive sewage released here in Duke City will be in Bethlehem by tomorrow, and in Help by Wednesday, and should arrive at The Pass early next week."

Another "chapter" was the Nuclear and Chemical Waste Watch. Plutonium had been detected in the grass at the zoo, and on the university soccer field. Its source was probably sewage sludge used as fertilizer. Sulfuric acid from old batteries leached into the ground water at many spots. And so forth.

Watch on Big River included a "chapter" called D.W.I. Watch. National and local statistics were compared and constantly updated. Deaths, injuries, medical costs, wreckage costs and resulting insurance rate increases were all listed regularly. Cost, sales, auctions and transfers of liquor licenses were publicized, startling the public. The debate linking D.W.I. to drive-up window liquor sales was kept on the air. Names and addresses of multiple offenders were obtained from the public record and read on the air. Victims and relatives of victims supplied a new wave of volunteers to the radio station.

There was a "chapter" called Burglary Watch. Statistics were aired, from the public record. The value of property reported stolen was constantly updated. Insurance cancellations were described. The debate on which sections of town were most vulnerable raged over the air, along with wide discussion of the effectiveness of what some condemned as "vigilante-ism." Names of fences, names of persons pleading guilty, details of plea bargains, and bail bond statistics all became part of Watch on Big River and its service to the community.

A Food Supply Watch became another "chapter." Food production in the county, and in nearby neighboring counties, growers' market information, food reserves available in local stores and warehouses compared to daily consumption rates — all went on the air. An ongoing debate raised general awareness of the phenomenon of hunger in Duke City.

That led to Homeless Watch. The program aired detailed information on shelters, shelter capacity and shelter use, meals, medical care, day care and other sources available, or sometimes not available, for homeless persons and families.

Robert instituted a Leukemia Watch, for personal reasons. He studied, and then aired, statistics by county. It became a study of prevailing wind currents. "Plutonium particles from The Cottonwoods should reach Holy Faith this afternoon, and will pass through The Meadows tomorrow morning."

And there was a Media Watch. KWBR aired daily analyses of the two local newspapers and their coverage of local news. Murders, prison overcrowding, the governor who didn't understand the function of the Legislative Branch, the Native American toll booth proposition — statistical summaries and highlights of the local news programs on the three TV stations were aired every day. There were on-going debates on censorship, on the phenomenon of the "pseudo-event," and on the practice of withholding names of perpetrators and victims on the basis of membership in one racial or ethnic group or another.

KWBR announced the votes of locally elected Federal officials. Patterns of absenteeism were noted. Discrepancies between public announcements and the actual facts of voting were also plainly pointed out. "Senator Jake announced that measles vaccine for all children in the U.S. would be nice, but that the country can't afford it. He smiled wanly when he was reminded that Cuba and Nicaragua can afford it. That same evening the Senator voted in favor of a new additional supply of nerve gas for the Pentagon, to replace the decomposing current stock, which must now be disposed of at great public expense."

The radio station developed a following, made up of those who think globally and want to act locally. Consternation grew also, among free-market profit-takers and military and commercial exploiters of the fragile environment. "Give us good news," became a complaint. Tourists who heard the station indicated that they took it to be satire, an extended joke.

Audience figures fluctuated. Many refused to listen. "I don't wanna know," became a refrain heard more often and more openly. But a faithful audience was building at the same time, and much of that audience became a pool of information volunteers. "Hey, did you hear what Senator Jake said at the Knights of Columbus last night —?"

Pressure began to build, not to clean up Duke City and correct problems, but to shut KWBR up altogether. Slap/nuisance law suits were tried, but the public outcry turned into unwanted negative publicity for the originators of the suits. Buy-out offers began coming in.

At last Robert accepted a buy-out offer he couldn't resist. He used the cash to buy another more powerful station.

◇   ◇   ◇

Undue Influence

Police and school officials are unable to hide their concern about the third suicide this week by a student at River Ranch High School. The school has hired a team of counsellors, who are available all through the school day, to talk with concerned students and faculty. A climate of fear has settled over the entire school. Police are studying the profile of each of the victims, two boys and a girl, from different parts of this suburban community, but have not yet found any pattern of clues.

Our reporter has interviewed several community leaders, to determine the reaction to this series of tragedies.

Police Chief: "It's obviously a case of someone being in the wrong place at the wrong time."

School Principle: "It's a very serious interruption of the academic and athletic life of the school. We do not, however, believe it reflects in any way on the character of our faculty or student body."

Local Priest: "Suicide is still a mortal sin, a form of murder in which the murderer cannot repent, because the murderer is at the same time the victim. The logic is unassailable."

Citizen: "All the media attention will only make matters worse. Why don't you all go away and leave us to grieve alone, with dignity?"

◇　◇　◇

A student reporter for the River Ranch High School newspaper has discovered that all four victims of the recent rash of suicides at the school were members of the same school club. During the "released time" free period, a Bible Study Club had formed recently. The adult advisor, a member of the local community, was Pastor Billy, of the local Second Advent

66

Church. The club has twenty-five members, or did have, before four of them committed suicide. The deaths occurred at different times and different places; it was not a group action. Our reporter has obtained permission to attend the next meeting of the club.

◇   ◇   ◇

Meetings of the Second Advent Bible Study Club have been canceled, until further notice, because of unfortunate publicity in connection with the recent series of suicides at the River Ranch High School. All the victims were members of the club.

◇   ◇   ◇

Our reporter attended Sunday Services at the Second Advent Church, where Pastor Billy presides. After the service, she spoke discreetly to several members of the flock, and then filed this report:

The persons attending the services told me that today's sermon was typical, that Pastor Billy preaches very often on the topic of Jesus' coming again, and heaven. One told me, "Our church isn't named Second Advent for nothing. The words mean that Jesus is coming again." The Bible texts refer to that belief, and the hymns sung by the congregation refer to it. Here are some especially pertinent sections:

"You will hear of wars and rumors of wars; see that you are not alarmed; for this must take place, but the end is not yet... Then will appear the sign of the Son of man in heaven, and then all the tribes of the earth will mourn, and they will see the Son of man coming on the clouds of heaven with power and great glory; and he will gather his elect from the four winds, from one end of heaven to the other... For as in those days before the flood they were eating and drinking, marrying and giving in marriage, until the day when Noah entered the ark, and they did not know until the flood came and swept them all away, so will be the coming of the Son of man. Then two men will be in the field; one is taken and one is left. Two men will be grinding at the mill; one is taken and one is left. Watch therefore, for you do

not know on what day your Lord is coming. "

"Let not your hearts be troubled; believe in God, believe also in me. In my Father's house are many mansions; if it were not so, I would have told you. I go to prepare a place for you. And when I go and prepare a place for you, I will come again and take you unto myself. "

"The Lord himself will descend from heaven with a cry of command, with the archangel's call, and with the sound of the trumpet of God. And the dead in Christ will rise first; then we who are alive, who are left, shall be caught up together with them in the clouds to meet the Lord in the air; and so we shall always be with the Lord. Therefore comfort one another with these words. "

Those are direct quotations from the Bible. And here are some verses from the hymns sung at the Second Advent Church:

"When all my labors and trials are o'er,
And I am safe on that beautiful shore,
Just to be near the dear Lord I adore,
Will through the ages be glory for me.
O that will be glory for me, glory for me, glory for me;
When by His grace I shall look on His face,
That will be glory, be glory for me. "

"In the land of fadeless day lies the city four-square,
It shall never pass away, and there is no night there.
God shall wipe away all tears;
There's no death, no pain, nor fears;
And they count not time by years,
For there is no night there. "

"There's a great day coming, a great day coming,
There's a great day coming by and by;

When the saints and the sinners
Shall be parted right and left.
Are you ready for that day to come?
Are you ready? Are you ready?
Are you ready for the judgment day?"

"Some glorious morning sorrow will cease,
Some glorious morning all will be peace;
Heartaches all ended, labor all done,
Heaven will open, Jesus will come.
Some golden daybreak Jesus will come;
Some golden daybreak, battles all won,
He'll shout the victory, break through the blue,
Some golden daybreak, for me, for you."

"When the trumpet of the Lord shall sound
And time shall be no more,
And the morning breaks eternal, bright and fair;
When the saved of earth shall gather
Over on the other shore,
And the roll is called up yonder, I'll be there."

"Shall we gather at the river,
Where bright angel feet have trod;
With its crystal tide forever
Flowing by the throne of God?
Ere we reach the shining river,
Lay we every burden down;
Grace our spirits will deliver,
And provide a robe and crown."

◇   ◇   ◇

We have obtained this interview with Pastor Billy, shortly after Sunday services at the Second Advent Church in River Ranch.

"Pastor Billy, would you agree with the idea that your

preaching and teaching is designed primarily to help people prepare to die?"

"My teaching is intended to bring people to the Lord, to be prepared to meet the Lord and his judgment. He is coming, and will surprise many people who are alive at this time."

"But — until he comes, the only other way to meet him is to die and go to where he is — is that right?"

"People who accept his grace, meet him immediately, find him present in their lives right now. You do *not* have to die to meet the Lord."

"Well, Pastor Billy, you mean that in — um, a spiritual sense, right? To be with him literally, he has to come, what you call his second advent, or the individual believer has to die. Isn't that right?"

"You, as an obvious unbeliever, use the word 'spiritual' to mean 'unreal.' I don't use it that way."

"Don't your sermons and the hymns your congregation sings place a great deal of emphasis on dying and heaven?"

"True believers are not afraid of dying. The Scriptures say they can take up poisonous serpents; they can eat poison, and not be harmed."

"What about radioactive materials? That's our modern poisonous serpent, our modern poison."

"True believers are not afraid of plutonium or atomic bombs. They fear God, and thus they fear nothing else."

"So, in your teaching, you're not concerned about nuclear war, or pollution, or extinction of species, or even the death of — of the Whole Thing?"

"The Lord will take care of his own."

"And the rest?"

"The rest is lost, already lost."

"The whales, the rain forest, the millions who worship God some other way, or not at all —"

"They are lost. All lost."

"I get the impression you don't love the world very much."

"The world is lost. I love the Lord."

"What do you think is the effect of your sermons on those who hear them?"

"I hope they bring unbelievers to the Lord, while there is still time."

"You're not worried about unstable adolescents misinterpreting what you say, what you repeat over and over, and coming to the wrong conclusions about it all?"

"Not really. God brings his own to himself, in his own way."

"You don't feel any responsibility for the six suicides that have taken place recently among members of your congregation?"

"How could I be responsible for what others do?"

"Your influence, your preaching — you don't think it causes results?"

"Sometimes the Lord gathers more of his precious flock to himself, through my work."

"And sometimes that looks to the world like suicide."

"The world is lost. Already lost. It doesn't matter to me what the world thinks, or what names the world uses for things."

"Has the Chief of Police talked to you about these suicides?"

"He has not."

◇　◇　◇

Our reporter has interviewed the Chief of Police in River Ranch, concerning the seven suicides by members of the Second Advent Club at the River Ranch High School, and filed this report:

The chief is unable at this time to tell us what action, if any may be taken against Pastor Billy, for possibly inciting, if not aiding and abetting, suicide. He told me that he had shared his files on the suicides with the County District Attorney, but refused to speculate on the likelihood of any legal action. He did indicate that in his personal opinion the pastor had wielded what the chief called "undue influence," over some of the high school students.

◇　◇　◇

Freewill, or Something

Gibb knelt to tend the fire in the fireplace and then stayed there, staring into the fire. He was silent and motionless for several minutes, lost in a sort of rapture, thinking, unaware of himself or what he was doing.

At last he moved, and got up stiffly. "Can you share it with me?" Teresa asked.

"Share what?" he said.

"What you were thinking. What you found out."

"Was I there long?"

"Long enough that I noticed," she said. "What was it?"

"Those same Big Questions. I was gone. In there. The Whole Thing. What's going on. The Bigger Picture. Decisions we make, or need to make. Putting it into words makes it a little scary. Time. How much time? Time running on and on. Time running out. Decisions to make. Default." He was almost back in trance.

"What decisions?" Teresa asked.

"I don't know." He snapped out of it. "Do you ever think like that? Like I just did?"

"Well, yes."

"What do you think?"

"About decisions?"

"About any of it," he said.

"I think we think we have choices. We think we make decisions, or need to make decisions. We feel proud sometimes and worried sometimes about our decisions and their consequences —"

"I worry more about delay in deciding, and the results of that," Gibb said.

"We think that we make decisions, that we have choices to make, but we really don't have free will at all," Teresa stated.

"You think that?" Gibb asked, a little surprised.

"Yes, I think that. There is an underlying Something, like a big interconnectedness — I don't know — which is always moving, very slowly. It makes things happen."

Gibb stared at her. "Interconnectedness," he echoed.

"Everything that we think is a decision," Teresa continued, "is really just some further movement of *That*. It does everything."

"'It,'" Gibb echoed. "Is It a machine?"

"Not exactly. Not just a big machine. More like a flow. Yes, a flowing. Moving all the time. Very slowly sometimes. Irresistibly."

"Inexorably," Gibb said, sounding a little desperate.

"Yes." Teresa smiled. "Inexorably. It does what it does. It does everything. And we are part of what It does. We aren't 'free' at all. We have no will at all. What feels like a decision on our part is It doing once again what it does." She smiled very sweetly.

"Where'd you get all that?" Gibb asked.

"Get all that? I didn't get all that anywhere. It's perfectly obvious. The great leaders of the world, the great heroes — they do their brief thing, and everyone cheers and worships and carries on. And It inches along a little further, and they are old and sick and feeble-minded and dead and lied about some more, and then forgotten. And It goes on, and on — inexorably."

"Is It alive? This thing that is doing everything?"

Teresa looked stumped, as if she'd never considered that, but only for a moment. "It isn't God, or a god. It is The Whole Thing."

"I see the idea. So it *is* alive. Part of what it does is produce what we call 'life.' Does It think? Does It have plans? Does It have free will?" Gibb asked.

"It isn't God."

"We agree on that," Gibb said. "I was just asking."

The telephone rang, and Teresa left the room to answer it. Gibb went on thinking. For example, Teresa makes a pie. The pie is for me, far more than for herself. She'll only eat a little of it. The pie, and the fact that she made it for me, delight me, and humble me. She does it to delight me, I think, but not to win points somehow with me, or It, or anyone or anything. She does it because that's an expression of what she is. She delights in delighting me that way.

Gibb recalled a conversation he and Teresa had had, more than once. What Teresa likes about me, she says, is that I allow her to be herself. I let her be who she is. But I tell her that that's easy, I can hardly take any credit for that. Because I *want* her to be what she is and as she is. That's what I love about her, that she *is* what she is and the way she is. Why would I want to interfere in any way? As if I really could, he then reminded himself.

Teresa returned to the fireside, where Gibb sat deep in thought. "It's some sort of underlying flow," she said. "I don't want to call it a machine. And I don't want to call it God. It's What There Is. All interconnected."

"Yes. I see it. I see it when I stare into the fire. Why does it make me feel so responsible for decisions?"

"I don't know," Teresa said, sounding a little sad. "It's a flow. It's an irresistible influence. A flowing. A flowing *in*."

"It flows through us," Gibb said, meaning it as a suggestion.

"Yes. We float in, or on, that flow." Teresa was also casting out freshly arrived-at notions.

"So our illusion about having a will, about being responsible, about having things to get up and go do — all of that is really It —"

"Your will is Its will," Teresa said. "It's not that you don't have a will, that you are just an acted-upon billiard ball on a cosmic pool table. You're part of that flow."

"I watch you," Gibb said. "You do go at it differently. You're not trying to push, the way I so often am. You're not trying to hinder either. You let it flow. Your free will is simply

Its irresistible determinism."

He thought deeply for a while, and she let him. "Maybe I'll learn this, yet," he murmured, at last.

She smiled. "It's inexorable," she said.

◇   ◇   ◇

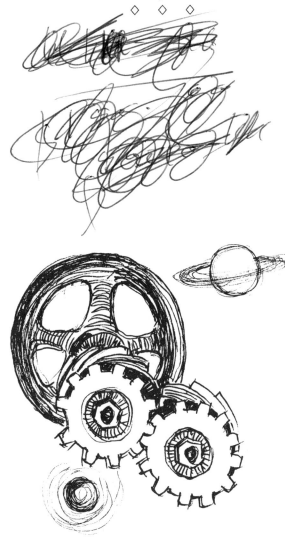

Report to Base

Bill and I have lived among this species for more than forty years. I appear to be one of them, and Bill has the form of a member of a common domesticated species — one that is allowed into the homes, and even into their beds and bathrooms. "They display a kind of modesty among themselves," Bill tells me, "which causes them to hide bodily functions like defecation and copulation from each other. But they hide nothing from the dog!" He has observed things which I have not, and has added very valuable insight into our investigation. I have watched the public arena, while Bill has been in a position to overhear the private side.

We do not age at a rate which they can perceive, and that presents a problem. The children Bill first played with are now grandparents and slowing down and becoming philosophical. This is good and bad, as far as our mission is concerned. We have had to move away and stay away a long while, and then when we return, I remain quite aloof. The family Bill lives with now, marvels at how much he resembles "Old Bill, who was lost in that hailstorm back in '52." He doesn't speak their language aloud to them, of course, so there's little danger that they'll catch on to the truth that he *is* Old Bill, and that we used that hailstorm as our excuse for separating from them before they became suspicious.

◇   ◇   ◇

Bill and I became part of a small town family in the industrial section of USA more than forty orbits ago. I didn't manifest as a fetus and then come to light by birthing, as a previous reconnaissance agent did a couple of millennia ago. Bill and I were adopted by a family, before careful and unchangeable records were kept. It would be harder to do now.

"He's here, so he's been born, and I'm adopting him as mine, so we want a birth certificate," my "father" explained to the young health department official. She typed it up and squeezed the raised-seal mechanism on the paper, which made it official, guaranteeing that I had been born, even though I hadn't. Bill, as a stray dog, had no trouble then, although he would have a more difficult time now, as records on pedigreed dogs are very meticulous, and strays are rounded up and exterminated.

The human species is moving toward rationality as regards stray dogs — they compete for food, they spread disease, they become sick and vicious and dangerous and perform no useful function. So they are being eliminated, gradually. At the same time the human attitude toward pedigreed dogs is moving away from rationality. They are of no practical use, except as emotional surrogates for family ties. They are very expensive and troublesome, and they are undependable as symbols of social prestige and rank, because fads in pedigrees change so rapidly and irrationally.

An extreme example of irrationality, as far as the human attitude toward dogs is concerned, can be seen in a recently developed breed, commonly called the "pit bull." Its evolution was controlled — something the humans have learned how to do so well that it looks like an instance of rationality, until we examine what they use their skills for. In the case of the pit bull they wanted to create a vicious fighting monster. The process has been quite successful, except that organized dog-fighting has been made almost universally illegal, and the damages caused by loose pit bulls who attack children, and even adult humans, has made some humans so angry that there are serious attempts now to have the pit bull declared an illegal substance. So far, sentiment ["Our family loves him so!" even though he just sent a young girl to the hospital] and economics ["I paid good money for that dog, more than a thousand bucks!"] have prevented any satisfactory resolution of this problem.

Anyway, Bill is a mongrel. But every time we have to move

a crisis arises for us. It would do our mission little good, if he simply stayed with me. Each time we must find a family which will adopt him, but then not watch over him so carefully and fretfully that he can't "escape" and confer with me periodically. That means he must evade "Animal Control" personnel and facilities. And the fact that he doesn't age perceptibly from the human vantage point makes it necessary for him to move from time to time.

◇ ◇ ◇

It's a good thing Bill and I were assigned to USA. That decision was made because the first nuclear explosion took place here and the second and third were prepared here and then carried to cities in Japan. We wanted to keep our eye on the most dangerous, and perhaps the farthest advanced, portion of the developing species.

Much of the culture of the entire species now comes from here, although some non-USA sectors of the species are not at all pleased about that. The language used here has become the *lingua franca* of the entire planet, not because it is a superior vehicle for communication, but because it was used by the dominant empires of the last two centuries. The music, the story-telling media, the stories [not the *best* stories, but the most widely disseminated stories] all come from here.

Japan might have been a good choice, also. USA was formerly the center of the world's wealth, but now Japan is. The two sectors are in serious competition and Japan is winning, largely because of the disparity in military spending.

This USA sector of the species consumes a highly disproportionate share of the resources of the world — raw materials, energy, products, even ideas. Everything is sucked into USA, and processed and used and used up and thrown away. Waste is rampant here, of organic material, of edible food, of usable clothing and tools. At the same time there is a growing sense of decline and scarcity, along with the general attitude that no one can do much about it.

◇ ◇ ◇

Many dozen million orbits ago the majority of the land animals on this planet were air-breathing reptiles, four-footed, cold-blooded, probably low in intelligence. They are extinct now. A few relatives survive — alligators and Komodo dragons and Galapagos lizards — but the dinosaurs, as the humans call them, are gone.

Human awareness of the previous existence of the dinosaurs is an interesting story. Myths of dragons are almost universal. Some of them could fly, some of them could breathe out fire, all were scaly yet reptilian, and usually they were the villains in the stories. The dragons seem remarkably like dinosaurs, even though there can be no direct memory. The dinosaurs were extinct millions of orbits before there were any humans.

Some curious humans found strange huge petrified bones, which had to have come from extinct animals. Myths which fixed the origin of the planet at a very recent date, and were being taken literally, hindered the comprehension of those old bones, called fossils. Even after comprehension became clear, many humans continued the literal use of the old myths. One told me, "The Devil put the fossils in the ground to deceive Man." When I asked him, using *his* myth, why God allowed the Devil to do that, he was stumped, but stuck to his explanation anyway.

After it became incontrovertible to all except the most inveterate literalists that the dinosaurs were real, in the sense that they had lived on the earth once and dominated all life forms for eons before dying out, what caused that extinction became a great source of debate. The small brain case in the dinosaur skeletons indicates a small brain, and may indicate lack of intelligence. For a long time the favorite explanation was that the stupid dinosaurs didn't have enough sense to protect their eggs, and that the much-smarter little mammals who were just appearing on the scene, ate too many dinosaur eggs, causing them to die out. It is pretty clearly a prejudiced theory, told by and for mammals. Humans and dogs are mammals. At any rate, the survivors of any great struggle always tell about it in such a way as to make themselves look good, or at least superior.

A later theory is that a sudden rash of volcanic, or perhaps meteoric, activity wiped out the vegetation, so that most of the animals then died, too. It is interesting, also, that another theory suggests that a sudden and inexplicable increase in cosmic radioactivity killed off many life forms and caused many sudden new mutations, creating new forms to replace those extincted. That theory is interesting to us, because the humans are themselves causing a huge sudden increase in radiation, preparing bombs and electricity in ways that they don't yet fully comprehend. Their bombs have the capacity to cause a vast increase in radio-activity, but the threat of self-extinction as a result of *that* is lost on the great majority of them.

We are now in a most peculiar phase in the human study of dinosaurs. The human children are fascinated by dinosaurs. Museums are built to cater to this obsession. Simplified but scientifically correct texts, and glorified fictional cartoon stories both contribute to the craze. For a while I wondered to myself, looking in display windows of children's bookstores, "They *love* dinosaurs. *Why* do they love dinosaurs so?"

I asked Bill, and he was quick with an answer. "All doomed species love dinosaurs." He may be on to something.

They have given them magical names: Thunder Lizard, King Tyrant, Roofed Lizard, Wing Finger, Three Horns. But now they are all gone. And now Knowing Man, as he calls himself, who may indeed know but doesn't *do* anything about what he knows, may join those who fascinate him so. I thought Bill was more hopeful than his proverb indicates, and certainly more hopeful than I, but his response was quick. The humans he's been living with lately may be a new discouragement to him that I don't yet fully comprehend.

◊   ◊   ◊

It is necessary to explain the nature of this report. All our observations have been transmitted to our home base planet immediately and instantaneously, as we make them, all of them, ever since our arrival here many orbits ago. The Intergalactic

Telepathic Network functions very well. What Bill and I see and hear can be seen and heard by any who wish to tune in at home, and our observations have been duly recorded. This report is more than a record of observations. It is intended to help observers at home understand better what can be seen and heard through us. Making sense of our observations can be very difficult for newcomers to the task of comprehending this planet. It certainly was for us, who are here. Conclusions may be drawn superficially and prematurely. Bill insists that I am still inclined to do exactly that, with reference to the humans, the most nearly intelligent species which we have studied so far. He sees things that I miss, he insists. Posing as one of their pets, he does observe things that I do not. Posing as one of them, I see the falseness and irrationality of their treatment of each other, and of me, and discount too quickly other qualities which Bill has spotted in them.

This report is being rendered in the information system which they call writing/reading. We have learned how it works. I am quite good at it. Bill can hardly write at all, for lack of practice. If they should catch him at it, it would cause trouble. He can read quite well, but has to be careful how and where and in whose presence he does it.

Humans have the capacity for telepathy, as do many of what they call the "lower" animals. The brain/organ is there, but they don't use it much. When telepathy does occur, they don't trust it. They only observe it after the fact, and marvel, but they haven't "harnessed" it at all, really. Some among them suspect that the invention of writing/reading has hindered the development of their telepathic skills.

They developed spoken language first, sounds made with the larynx, shaped by lips and tongue and teeth. Scholars who have studied our immediate intergalactic telepathic communications have watched me using this "speech," as the humans call it. Bill does not use it, so as not to risk exposing our disguises. They have myths and nursery rhymes about talking dogs, but the real thing would alarm them greatly.

After eons they learned to make marks which represent the spoken language. It is really quite remarkable. Sometimes the marks are stylized pictures, and there is one family of written languages which depends on that fact. But mostly the marks have come to represent sounds, and they make these marks more or less in the order in which they make the sounds. Some systems are much more consistent about this than others. The dominant language, the one being used in this report, is *not* notably consistent in this regard. At any rate, another human can come along later, sometimes much much later, and if he knows that set of marks and that spoken language, he can look at the marks and "read" them, and hear again the inner speech of the one who wrote them. The invention impresses us greatly, and we have gone to much trouble to learn how to use it.

The marks can survive the one who made them, and preserve his speech, or his thoughts. The marks have been preserved in many different ways — painting on stone walls, carving into granite or marble, impressions on mud pies which are later baked, painting on animal skins. The most commonly used invention is very thin light-colored sheets of material derived mostly from the crushed bodies of trees, on which the marks can be made with colored liquid, or scratched with a pointed instrument which leaves a colored scar.

Whoever is monitoring my visual impressions right now can see the marks I am making across this paper. I wonder if anyone there has "learned" this language well enough to make sense of the marks I'm making, as I make them. If not, this report will constitute reason to begin doing so at once.

We have learned how this invention works, and have decided that I should prepare this record. It is not exactly an addition to my report to headquarters, although headquarters will have it, because my observations are focused on this record, while I am preparing it. One of their writers asks, in a play that deals with censorship, "Can a person write a book without reading it?"

This report, or record, will contain in preservable form, my thoughts about my own observations. The two things are different. The report will be preserved here, like their own records, hidden among their records, probably as "fiction," meaning that it's a made-up story. Bill and I are mythological to them, or would be, if they knew about us. Their librarians will call this report "science fiction." "Science" is their word for the amassed knowledge which they regard as "proven," even though it isn't. Their phrase "science fiction" is a contradiction in terms. They use many of them and I take pleasure in collecting them. "Science fiction" means "proven fact/not fact." Much science fiction is set in the future, often trying to imagine where their technology is taking them, extrapolating all too often their obsession with fighting and conquest, imagining the possibilities that they'll never get to see. This report, of a visit from outside the galaxy, will be taken as fiction, and if taken seriously at all, as science fiction. So be it.

Meanwhile, I use this invention to go deeper into pondering and analysis and synthesis. I prolong thereby our final decision concerning our assignment and our findings. I learn meanwhile to think more and more like them. Maybe I'll come to understand them better. Bill hopes so.

◊   ◊   ◊

We were sent here to ascertain whether there is intelligent life on this planet. Radio signals and nuclear explosions seemed to indicate the possibility. We aren't sure yet. At times it appears obvious, because one species *has* indeed discovered important facts about matter and energy and invented some remarkable devices. And several other species display impressive skill at learning from experience. Even dogs can do it, as Bill is pleased to remind any who will, or can, listen to him. Bill was the one who told me about Pavlov's experiments, which proved that dogs can learn, even though that isn't exactly what Pavlov made out of his findings.

But that same inventive species, I mean the human, does not behave intelligently. It is as though intelligence were some kind of part-time game, a part-time employment at best, but not something to be lived by. Almost all the members of that species live by egotism and inherited bodily fear and an unwise search for instant gratification of irrational desires, some of which deal with things that are totally imaginary.

Yet this very same species has come upon the *idea* of intelligence. The word is in their dictionaries, and their books of philosophy. That word means, "The love of wisdom," and is not necessarily quite the same thing as intelligence. It is one of their fields of scholarly specialization. It has lately become hard to define philosophy, now that mathematics, physics, biochemistry, military strategy and hundreds of other specialties have split away from it. Sometimes it appears that what's left of philosophy is the analysis of what thinking is, or is for. How thinking works is the domain of psychology and neuro-anatomy, and lately of the new field called "computer science and artificial intelligence," but what thinking, and living, are *for* is left to philosophy. And modern philosophers are not doing anything very impressive with the question, if I can tell from what they say and write.

The humans ask themselves, "What is intelligence?" They ponder the possibility of intelligence on other planets, but not very seriously as yet. That's mostly science fiction, to them. A few suspect a marvelous intelligence in their own oceans, among certain marine mammals, but they seem singularly unimpressed by the possibility, and continue slaughtering those beings for no good reason. Of course, they have done the very same thing to their own species, sometimes on a grand scale. Bill is upset that so many carcasses of those obviously nearly intelligent marine animals end up as dog food. I ask him, "If the ocean animals are so intelligent, why can't they somehow end the slaughter?" Bill doesn't know.

"What is intelligence?" their philosophers ask. Speech, the ability to reason, the ability to remember, the ability to learn, the ability to solve problems — these all contribute to what they call intelligence.

This species has speech. However, the ability is tainted by the fact that it is used all too often to deceive, to lie, "to say that which is not," as one of their greatest writers put it, in a book called, *THE TRAVELS OF LEMUEL GULLIVER.*

Sometimes they can reason, but they don't do it much in their practical lives. Reason turns up mostly in games, not life. Chess and bridge are two prominent reasoning games. Persons who are very skilled, play the game in rooms filled with smoke and go home to unhappy marriages and unsatisfactory jobs, which they cannot reason their way out of. It's as if they were half-intelligent.

They can remember, but once again, they don't much, or at least not in areas that matter. Wall Street gamblers do not remember the Stock Market Crash of 1929. World conquerors do not remember Waterloo or Stalingrad. History is an enterprise among them, but ignored by governments and voters and draftees. One of their scholars, in the field of history, said, "What I learn from the study of history is that humans do not learn anything from the study of history." They do not use memory intelligently.

They can learn in the sense of mastering new skills quickly. But they do not learn to see patterns in their individual, or collective, lives. They solve problems, but none of the problems are very important. They use the inventions they come up with to enhance their greediness and their egotism and their sense of superiority over others. And now that their inventions are capable of destroying them, they refuse to regard *that* as the greatest danger confronting them.

They have a remarkable mental ability to put facts out of their consciousness, to refuse to relate one fact to another, if the resulting insight is unpleasant for the individual. "I'll think about that tomorrow," said one of their more fatuous heroines in a very popular story about one of their most bloody and unnecessary wars. "Don't disturb me with the facts," is one of their proverbs. "Ignorance is bliss," is another.

Examining their dictionaries can reveal much. "Intelligence: the ability to learn or understand from experience; the ability to acquire and retain knowledge; the ability to respond quickly and successfully to a new situation; the use of the faculty of reason in solving problems; directing conduct effectively..." We note their pride in their problem-solving ability, and their consistent failure in directing their own individual conduct effectively.

There is another more recent definition of intelligence, which leads to one of those comic accidents of their language. The word "intelligence" can mean "military secrets, information provided by spies and hired assassins." This kind of "intelligence" has been found to be wrong and misused so much in recent decades that "military intelligence" is now regarded among the more aware among them as one more contradiction in terms.

◇ ◇ ◇

The human use of language, which at first glance appears to be a tool for reason, and for communicating rationally, is now as often as not a contributing factor in their irrational behavior. Large numbers of them have forgotten the meanings of their own words. For example, one will say, "How do you account for Such-and-such and Thus-and-so happening at the same time?"

And another will answer, "Oh, I'm sure that was just a co-incidence," thinking that he has given a meaningful, even rational, reply.

They have both forgotten that the word "co-incidence" is derived from Latin and means, "events occurring at the same time," "occurring together." But the first one already had that in his question. "How about these two events that occurred together?" To say, "Oh, they're events that occurred together," is not to give a sensible, much less rational, answer.

They do a great deal of this, and much of the time they are not aware that they are not saying anything. They even think this kind of conversation is useful in problem solving and decision making. It isn't, and their tentative steps toward rational thinking and rational behavior are nipped in the bud.

It took Bill and me a while to comprehend how feeble this tool is in the hands, or rather the mouths, of this species. We, of course, have telepathy for communication. We use our version of spoken speech to *do* things, effect things, create things, *cause* things to happen. They have old myths that use language that way, but it does not happen in reality. "Let there be light," and there was light. "Peace! Be still!" and there was a great calm. "Swallow that man!" and a great fish swallowed him. "Be healed," and the leprosy left him. The presence of these stories in their mythology seems to have no effect on how they understand and use their language.

I remember when I first began to suspect how feeble their language really is. Boys were playing in a field, digging, pretending to be fugitives burying secret treasure. Or perhaps they were digging up an old treasure buried earlier. Bill sniffed and pawed the ground and poked into their hole. I watched. Since I hadn't mastered their speech yet, they thought of me as a foreigner, and mostly ignored me.

At one point Bill got in the way of the one digging. He poked the shovel at Bill and growled, "Get away, damn it." I had learned the word "damn," meaning a curse, an eternal condemnation, but I didn't know what "it" referred to in the boy's sentence. I was studying the scene and the words carefully. Bill thought the digger was playing with him. He wagged his stump of a tail and jumped toward the shovel.

"Damn you!" shouted the boy. I was expecting a thunderbolt from the sky, or a gaping hole to open under Bill and swallow him, or burning fire to break out in his fur — but, no. Nothing. The boy condemned him, but we could notice no change.

One of the other boys said to the one with the shovel, "Take it easy, Rocky! He's just playing."

Later Bill and I conferred about it. Bill had already figured it out. "Their talking doesn't work. They speak and nothing happens."

◇   ◇   ◇

It is remarkable how much direct blatant contradiction occurs in their public conversations. Absolutely nonsensical sentences are pronounced every few moments. I have heard and recorded these myself:

"He's seventy-four, but I don't know how old he is."

"It's boring, but some of it is interesting."

"I'm not saying slick is especially good, but it's not slick enough."

Sometimes the word "but" in these sentences seems to indicate merely: "I'm now going to take back what I just said, and you won't be able to disagree with me." To say the least, this use of language is irrational.

Sometimes the contradiction seems to be deep in the mind, based on the irrational assumption that the speaker and his group are good, and others are bad. "There'd be less terrorism in the world, if we did more of it." The speaker was defending acts of arson and murder by the secret spy agency on his side in world conflict, and didn't see how similar such acts are, no matter which side perpetrates them. It is very typical of this species.

The publicly disseminated "news," in which powerful officials tell the general public what to believe and what to think, is rife with this same kind of non-communication:

"The corporation gained ten billion dollars last year in profits, and so could not afford to offer the labor force any raises in the new contract."

"Seventy thousand miles of wilderness beaches have been covered with oil, but the spill was not caused by anyone and no one is at fault."

"Colonel So-and-so stated that he had deliberately lied to the Congress, but the judge has ruled that he was not guilty of perjury."

The advertisements for products to buy, which are interspersed with the same "news" announcements, also contain blatantly marvelous contradictions:

"This pill will take away the headache caused by the soundtrack portion of this advertisement."

"This drug will age you faster and make you feel good about it at the same time."

"This drug will make you exempt from the aging process which characterizes all life and all existence in this sector of the galaxy."

"This car will enable you to break without effort and with impunity all the laws against speeding and reckless driving in all fifty states."

Sometimes the words are not spelled out as I am doing in this account, but the juxtaposition of words and pictures constitutes the contradiction and reveals it.

Ordinary conversations which Bill and I have overheard are full of statements which contradict each other and known facts. One of their scientists made a study of these instances of erroneous speech and called it, *THE PSYCHOLOGY OF ERRORS*. Since then a certain kind of slip of the lip has been named for him.

A Vice-president of the nation said, "We're making great strides in the elimination of human rights in El Salvador." The news commentator corrected him, saying that he meant to say "the preservation" of human rights in that war-ravaged country, but Dr. Freud's insight indicates otherwise. Sometimes humans state the pure truth, saying exactly what they mean, and meaning exactly what they say, albeit unintentionally. The vice-president intended to lie, but on this rare occasion, didn't.

Earlier, a President made several such slips in the same State of the Union speech. He was such a non-stop liar, that it became a joke in the land. "Thanks to Dr. Freud, the truth leaks out, in spite of everything."

The inveterate use of contradiction leads quickly to lying. We have observed that the opposite is also true. A rational being, like Bill or me, can spot lying quickly. One government official was upset that an individual congressperson had gone into the Central American war zone without the sanction of the War Department. [They call that the "Defense Department," having begun to do so just after it ceased being defense and became planetary aggression.] The official lamented to the public the unauthorized trip by the congressperson, saying, "He's upsetting the Peace Plan!" But we all could tell that he really meant, "He's upsetting the official, secret War Plan!"

◊ ◊ ◊

Some humans report that writing helps clarify thought, contributing to rationality. Many nearly rational books have been written by humans. Of course, many irrational ones have been written also. The difficulty for us observers is that some humans have the *idea* of rationality quite clearly worked out, but then we look in vain for rational behavior. Mostly writing is an extension of speech, especially lately when it's easy to do with cheap pens and paper and even easier with computer word-processors. When it was done by carving symbols in granite, or by poking mudpies with sticks and then baking the pies, writing was less trivial than it's become lately.

Many humans do not read or write. More read than write. Among those who do read and write, the percentage of those who indulge in rational behavior is about the same as among those that do not read or write and likewise among those that do not know *how* to read or write. The percentage is a tiny number, just a little larger than zero.

At times, although not at all times by any means, the words, spoken or written, appear rational. But then the actions of the speaker or writer do not. Thus our preliminary conclusion, "Pre-rational." They even have a proverb: "Actions speak louder than words." It is quite remarkable — it appears that some of them, at least, are aware of this inconsistency.

Reason will effect behavior, if it *is* reason. A rational stated intention is not the same as rational behavior. A rational post-datum explanation, which they even have sufficient clarity to call a "rationalization," is not rational behavior. They do seem to want their behavior to *appear* rational — hence we hear rationalizations, but it is not made rational on that account.

Our preliminary evaluation is based on what we have observed them doing. They have the ability to develop a remarkable degree of comprehension of how a thing works, how a process can be altered, how things are, *how it is*. But then the person behaves as if he did *not* have that understanding.

We watched a human jump into a car which was rolling slowly

toward a precipice in a national park. He went over the edge of the precipice in the car and was killed. I asked the human standing next to me to explain the dead human's behavior. "Oh, he just bought it," he told me. "Evidently the emergency brake didn't hold. He must have thought he could save it. What a tragedy!"

When I stated that he was irrationally attached to his possessions and is now dead as a result, a crowd gathered and was prepared to blame *me* for the death. That's how irrational they are capable of being. Bill and I were glad to get away.

Humans have a remarkable ability to repair mechanical things How does it work? What's the matter with it now? By reason and intuition they find the loose wire, the worn-out insulation, the broken bearing. They can use the process of elimination perfectly in unimportant areas. They have remarkable powers of memory, although these have been weakened by the invention and growing use of writing and the computer.

Yet in important areas they do not do well. Marriage, child rearing, the causes of war, the causes of economic scarcity, the application of safety measures which eat into profits — they appear downright stupid.

For example, there is a town where the ground water has been poisoned by a large manufacturing firm. All humans need clean water, to drink and bathe in, in order to survive. The evidence is in — collected in a rational manner. The poison from the factory is causing illness and death. Yet the people continue to live there, and the firm continues to pollute the water. Rationalizations for the irrational behavior include, "We don't want to lose our jobs." "The clean-up will cost too much." "The proof isn't scientific."

One could argue that the poison which causes illness and death also causes mental malfunction. It is possible. *All* the air and water on the planet is polluted to some degree already.

◇   ◇   ◇

It is now clear that it was a mistake on our part to materialize Bill as a dog. Dogs are a non-rational species, domesticated by humans a dozen thousand orbits ago, that is, fairly recently. The dog's instincts have been somewhat humanized, but there is no process of rational thought. At best there is a kind of slave mentality, with the dog wanting so much to please the master, no matter what abuse may be meted out. Those dogs that don't display much of this fawning, hand-licking obedience simply run away, and most of them are killed by machines which the humans have made to move around in.

Another domestic animal which shows surprisingly less of this slave attitude is the cat. We began to notice this when someone in the family Bill was staying with remarked, "That dog behaves more like a cat than a dog!" Bill has to work hard at pretending to want to please the humans. His true feelings are usually somewhere between disdain and disgust, or at least they were early on in our observations. Cats behave exactly that way, tolerating touching only when *they* are in the mood, not obeying *at all,* making use of the arrangement only if it suits the cat and brings some advantage to the cat, like warmth and unearned food. We've often wondered what the humans get out of the domestication of the cat. A strange sort of aloof companionship for the lonely humans results, but certainly no abject obedience, and little obvious advantage.

At any rate Bill's function has been to use his guise as a dog to spy on the humans. We would have learned much more about rationality as such on this planet, if he had materialized here as a dolphin. He and I would have had much less pleasant direct contact with each other, to be sure, since humans and dolphins seldom meet. But whenever we could contrive to meet, at one of their maritime circuses or study institutes, where dolphins are kept prisoner and studied and made to entertain crowds, we would have had much more to tell each other about the process of rational thought on this planet.

The mistake was natural enough, given the distances involved in our preliminary observations. Humans live above the surface, breathe air, cut down trees, build houses and cities. They dig holes into the earth and recently have begun to build conveyances that carry them over land, over water, under water, and in the air and beyond their atmosphere. A few have been to their moon. Dogs accompany humans in their homes, on the surface of the ground, breathing air. They used to be useful in hunting or herding other animals, but those activities are very rare now. The dog's function, we've come to see, is mostly sentimental, to satisfy their need for unconditional and irrational approval.

Dolphins breathe air, but live exclusively in the water. The fact that they are as nearly rational as the humans, and perhaps more so, is hard to perceive at first. Very few humans have perceived it. Dolphins do not alter the environment, except to eat several fish each per day. They do not disturb coral, dig holes, pollute the water they live in, or build artifacts of any kind. This last is what fooled us. A rational species that does not make tools or leave records is rare. Yet there may be one on this planet. I strongly recommend additional study, while there is still time. The humans are killing the dolphins, for no very clear reason, at an astounding rate.

Dolphins have a remarkably complex language and unwritten lore. We have learned some of this visiting the seacoast and using our telepathic powers. Poetry and saga and remembered lists are extremely impressive. And, in contrast to the humans, they are no threat to the life system they are part of. On that account alone they appear to be more rational than the humans, who are a threat not only to dolphins but to all living things and the very life process itself. Concern about that is what brought us here and keeps us here.

Let's clear up immediately the reason for our coming. The three nuclear explosions that attracted our attention to this sector of the galaxy in the first place — during the orbit they number 1945 — were not laboratory accidents. They were set off deliberately — two of them with a view to inflicting injury on fellow humans, and the first as an experiment to see if the device would work at all. Two human traits which have not been controlled by rationality or by anything else are plainly visible in these early atomic incidents: curiosity and ferocity.

◊   ◊   ◊

Our preliminary judgment is that the species is pre-rational. We know of no other species that has spent so long a period in this intermediary stage, but perhaps the Galactic Librarians do. Some of the individual organisms are capable of rational thought. The feats of inference, quantification and substantiation in certain individuals is undeniably impressive. They have invented several methods of storing information for use by other individuals later, perhaps much later. A body of knowledge is being built up. A dependable method of testing knowledge, new and old, is widely accepted by the knowledge experts in all parts of the globe.

The existence of knowledge experts may be the crux of the matter, forcing us to evaluate this species as pre-rational. Some of them can think rationally. Very few individuals, and no groups as yet discovered, are capable of acting rationally. It may not be a question of ability, to be sure; we give a statistical summary only. In no known case has one of them been found to *behave* consistently in a rational manner. Those very few who have come close to dependably rational behavior are in every case regarded as mad, or in some way superhuman or divine. The myth of the totally rational person does exist, but the observable fact does not.

Bill and I have had to learn how to dissimulate, feigning something like that stupidity which they all display, for fear that our disguises and perhaps something of our true nature and mission would be exposed. We certainly don't want the role of any of their Messiahs — the record consistently indicates that that is always very dangerous.

A couple of examples will make clear how irrational behavior undercuts the seeming ability to do rational thinking. Humans have made remarkable strides in their comprehension of numbers. They work with positive, negative, hypothetical and even imaginary numbers. They organize huge enterprises, intercontinental in scope, on the basis of their mastery of numbers. They teach their number lore to the very young, and reward well those who become number specialists.

But, with all this mastery of the concept of number, they elect as Chief Magistrate, in charge of the largest single budget on the planet and in charge of all expenditures, a man who does not comprehend the idea of the negative number. He then subtracts hugely from income and adds enormously to outgo, and denies that the result is a negative number, which they call a "deficit." He simply denies it, because he doesn't understand it, and all the others, many of whom *do* understand it at some level at least, allow him to do it and keep on doing it.

Another example can be seen in the human reaction to the destruction of the ozone layer which shields the surface of the planet from the most intense solar and cosmic radiation. This shield, which took hundreds of millions of orbits to form, and made possible the evolution of life forms in the atmosphere unprotected by the water in which life first appeared, is understood by most humans. The knowledge specialists understand it very well, remarkably well, in detail, having made astounding observations and measurements and good inferences. The rest of the population understand it in a general sense.

But, with all this rational understanding, which includes clear knowledge of the causes of the ongoing depletion of the ozone layer, the humans cannot decide to deal rationally with those causes. Certain chemicals involved in the use of items as diverse as refrigerants and hair-stiffeners, designed to keep their hair in place in wind and strenuous activity — mostly a vanity concern, which we didn't comprehend at first — rise above the atmosphere after use and degrade chemically the ozone. But people value these products, and their manufacturers insist on the profits they are making. So, even though skin cancer and other results of excess solar radiation are on the increase, in a measurably striking curve, the humans can only take inept steps at doing away with the cause. "New standards," to be applied only gradually, and only "next decade," are talked about. Little or nothing is really done.

This species, as a whole, fails in the doing. Remarkable

individuals stand out, sometimes, but the entire group drifts toward disaster, totally unaided by rationality.

◇   ◇   ◇

Some members of the human species are trying to build machines that can think rationally. Artificial Intelligence, shortened to A-I, is their phrase for it. It is quite a remarkable development, since so few of the species themselves think rationally and none behave rationally. The machine-builders have given up on training or educating their fellow humans to think. Machines are easier to work with, they say.

Our first observations of this new wrinkle surprised us. It appeared that the humans could and did make machines that were more rational than they. Binary numbers are at the heart of it, yes-or-no questions, punched or unpunched holes in cards at first, then open or closed electronic switches. Mathematical calculations are greatly speeded up and what looks like reasoning is enhanced, often in extremely round-about fashion. Telepathy is much easier, from our point of view.

The irrationality of the machine operator is often exposed. I have heard computer operators stop pressing the keyboard and glare and then shout at the screen, "But that's not what I meant, you Idiot!" The machine does exactly what it is instructed to do, and does not waste time trying to read the operator's mind — indeed, it cannot. "This goddam machine is dumb as a stick!" the same irrational operator declared. It was a marvelous redundancy. We do not see how irrational beings could create rational machines.

Reason can come out of the mechanical process they have set up, if nothing but reason ever goes in, and there are no slip-ups which the machine will not bother to catch. The humans have the clue in their slogan, "Garbage in, garbage out." There was an earlier versicle, not intended for calculators and computers, but for mythological entities, but applicable nevertheless. "God is not mocked. Whatsoever a man soweth, that shall he also reap."

The so-called thinking machines do exactly what they are told, no matter what was "meant." They do not think thoughts. They "run programs" that are punched into them, but they do not "invent" things. This pre-rational species will not be made rational by the computer.

In fact, the computer may become a hindrance to the hoped-for human evolution into rational behavior. The computer, like its maker, fails our test. It may "think" pre-programmed rational "thoughts," but it doesn't act at all. It only obeys.

Some questionable human actions are already being blamed on the computer. It amounts to a type of rationalization, not unlike that medieval alibi, "The Devil made me do it!"

One human did some work for a huge corporation and was owed payment for his work. No check was forthcoming. When he called the office to enquire about his compensation for work done, he was told that the computer could only write checks on the 24th day of the month. When he called on the 29th, noting that he still had no check, he was told that the computer was "down." When he called again he was reminded that the computer would be writing checks again on the 24th of the following month. Several months went by. He finally sued the company and its computer, saying, "I have a computer myself. I plug it in and turn it on, and I can make it do whatever I want it to do, at any time of the day or night, on any day of the month. My computer obeys me. You folks need a new, more obedient computer."

Actually, they did not. Their computer was doing exactly what someone had instructed it to do, and the person answering the phone and casting all the blame on the computer was doing exactly what *she* was instructed to do, also, and the intention, which was to keep and use the man's money for as long as possible, was being executed perfectly. The proof was that the company did not want to engage its expensive lawyers in such a small matter, so the check came through before the court date, and not written on the 24th day of the month after all.

Much more serious matters are being turned over to computers, with the assumption that they are rational and safe. "Fail-safe" is an ironic phrase which some of them bandy back and forth. But in fact, when to bomb whom, with what and with how much and how often, what dose of what drug to administer and to whom, how much to charge for this product or that service, and whom to blame for whatever — all these are human decisions, made by humans, not computers.

◇   ◇   ◇

Some humans use a very peculiar method of thinking. Whole schools have been built up around it, developing factions which are prepared to fight each other, and even wage total war upon each other. The humans tell themselves that all the fighting over such matters is in the past, but it is not.

They take completely untestable axioms, and using them as a base, proceed to logic, with its use of inference, deduction, induction and all the tools and rules of rational thinking. This is called among them, "Theology."

The untestable axioms are widely varied. For example: that there are "higher" beings invisible, but powerful, called angels and/or devils and/or gods. Or, that there is only one higher being, called by hundreds of various names. Or, that this higher being became a human. Or, that this higher being has a favorite human group and all others are inferior in some way. Or, that this higher being which became human suffered and died as humans do, and that that somehow benefitted all humans. Totally untestable, all of it. Of marginal interest, perhaps, to many. Of interest to us because of the extremely bizarre conclusions that have been arrived at by applying "reason" to those preposterous axioms.

Some theologians, a minority of the total, have arrived at conclusions that are quite admirable and even reasonable. For example: that the higher being can reveal itself or express itself through any human individual or group, or any other vehicle. Or, that it is a bad thing to use this theology to advance one's own group or one's own private gain. Or, that it is a serious ethical question to dedicate human energy and ingenuity to the building of mechanisms which are capable of destroying all human life and perhaps the very process of Life itself.

Other theologians can use the same logic and the same unprovable axioms about higher beings to prove that one's own group is superior, or that one individual human is equivalent to the higher being itself, or that some racial groups are inferior to others, or that government officials execute in any and all instances the will of the higher being, or that mass murder is no crime if done in the name of the higher being.

The theologians provide the mental ammunition to fuel most of the slaughter/frenzies of the humans, and it has been thus for many centuries. Crusades, genocidal extermination efforts, persecution of minorities — all this peculiarly human activity has been made more nasty than it would otherwise have been by the rationalization and justification and fomentation of those most murderous instincts and activities, by the theologians. It amounts to using logic to make the violent tendencies of humans worse than they would otherwise be.

◇   ◇   ◇

Bill and I get into some remarkable "discussions" when we are able to spend time alone together. Our interaction is telepathic, of course. He doesn't have the lip and tongue control, in his disguise as a dog, to be able to speak well in any human language, including the one that I have learned. So we fire thoughts at each other quite vociferously.

We were in my quarters, in the home of the family I was staying with. We were looking at educational videos, remarkable photography of remarkable details, taken by human specialists. First an ant hill. Then a bee hive. We agree that there is some kind of collective intelligence at work in both places, capable of food gathering, caring for the queen, nurturing the larvae, disposing of the dead — but problem-solving seems to be random and almost statistical, and wider awareness seems entirely lacking. We need to keep our eye on this tendency toward intelligence, but it has nothing directly to do with those signals which brought us here originally, namely atomic explosions.

We watched pictures of dolphins, romping together in the sea. We have already reported the preliminary indications of intelligence, especially language. If they are intelligent, however, they seem to be doing little with it, other than enjoying being alive. But that *is* intelligent behavior, we both agree. Perhaps I am slightly infected with the human way of thinking, that everything should be for some other purpose, not for what it is in itself. At any rate, the questions about dolphin intelligence center around their inability to defend themselves against the incessant attacks on them from humans. They need to put their intelligence to work, it would seem. They have never invented anything like a weapon.

Then we looked at pictures of the humans. One of their knowledge persons referred to his own species as "the naked ape," referring to the primate group which humans evolved from, and ignoring the almost universal human tendency to wear clothes, or at least decorations. We decided to seek pictures of humans naked. They seemed to be scarce at first, such pictures, but are not really, if one knows where to look. Of course, Bill sees them naked quite often — all their pretended modesty goes away when they are alone with the dog.

We found some pictures. I must admit to being fascinated. Bill was bored, and then became indignant at my curiosity. Of course, he has seen them copulating many times, has seen all their foreplay and finds it lacking in interest or importance. I was studying pictures of some kind of group gathering, of "naked apes." Bill asked, "That's a sign of intelligence?"

"Not as such," I had to admit, "but I find it very interesting."

"It is only mildly interesting. It is *not* intelligence. It is Mindless Drive, left over from a period when they needed to increase their numbers in order to survive the predators that ate them and the diseases that killed them off young. At this stage in the development of the species, such unrestrained and uncontrolled copulation is a sign of a *lack* of intelligence."

I had to agree. But I remained fascinated by the pictures we had found. Bill continued his tirade. "It is Desire; it is misguided Instinct. Maybe it is Love, although I doubt it, in such a group setting. If we're looking for intelligence, we won't find it here."

◇   ◇   ◇

The question becomes more and more urgent: Can this species learn to care enough about itself *as a species,* soon enough, to refrain from polluting the surface of this entire planet to such a degree that no life forms can survive? If not, perhaps we should conclude this mission, call it "Not-intelligent" and be done with it, and get away now. The planet is rapidly becoming poisonous to *them,* not counting the radioactivity which is leaking from their every attempt to tamper with nuclear energy. The poison may be harming us in ways that we are not aware of. The danger of total irradiation, by the explosion of dozens of thousands of nuclear bombs, is very real. An accident, a mistaken set of instructions given to their computers, a maniac turned loose, or some other totally unforeseeable development could make this planet uninhabitable by any life forms whatever.

Our instructions are not to interfere, and we have been very scrupulous about not doing so. I do admit to being tempted to help those of the human species who want to dismantle and destroy the wherewithal to blow away the Web of Life itself. The Web has been in development for a long time, and will no doubt finally produce intelligence, if it's not destroyed first.

We are learning to think of a bee hive or an ant colony as a single multi-celled organism. Each hive or colony is "pre-rational." Perhaps humanity could be thought of in a similar way, although there is not any kind of coherent group which would correspond to a "hive." Their nations, which take up most of their weak sense of loyalty, are far too large, their cities too crowded and not self-sufficient, their towns too divided along racial and religious and social-rank lines.

If we think of the whole species as one organism, we wonder what to make of recent developments. Decisions are made by remarkably few of the individuals, and lately those decisions have all been markedly unintelligent. For example: the decisions to assemble all this explosive and poisonous material, and the current inability to make the required decision to stop making more of it and remove what is now polluting the planet.

◇   ◇   ◇

We went back to the videos of the bee hives. The individual bee seems to be totally unaware of herself as a separate entity. She will attack an intruder, bury her stinger and all the contents of her abdomen in any intruder, with no hesitation. She will work herself to death and doesn't need to be lured or threatened or forced or persuaded to do so.

In contrast, individual humans have a awareness of themselves as separate individuals. This sense is called "ego." It has to be trained out of them, to make soldiers of them, for example, and even so, ego sometimes gets in the way of individual heroism, especially if the leaders are lying cowards, which has often been the case recently. Workers need to have ego redirected, into a kind of altruism, so they'll be willing to suffer abuse and privation and exhaustion "for the family." Women workers have been taught to override ego altogether. Young unattached male workers are the hardest to manage, from the point of view of employers — they are quickest to strike, to walk away in disgust, to commit acts of destructive violence.

This sense of ego in humans is a marvelous invention. Each one, unless damaged, has a sense of "I," of separateness, of responsibility for personal consequences. This "ego" gets things done and moves activity out into new areas. "I will do it myself." "Who will do it, if I shirk, or fail?" ego says.

There is a difficulty. This ego-thing makes the mortality of the individual human a problem. Unlike the bee, the individual can foresee his or her own death. It is almost universally thought of as a bad thing. The healers among them are at this time totally obsessed with the irrational idea that Death is an Enemy to be combatted, and even overcome. When the physician finally turns away from the dying patient, he feels defeated. And, of course, he *is* defeated every time. There is no known case of a human not dying, finally. The ego-sense makes both patient and doctor irrational. The patient thinks it is unfair that he or she must die, and the doctor thinks it is his duty to defeat an unavoidable, irresistible process.

This mixture of ego and mortality has created art among the humans. No other animal has it. The bees build their hives around the hexagonal-solid shape of their individual cells. The ants build colonies of mud and underground tunnels and chambers. Birds build nests. But the humans build all kinds of structures, absolutely everywhere, and pave everything else. Also they create all kinds of non-utilitarian objects, and decorate the useful ones needlessly, constantly leaving their mark. They carve their initials on what few trees are left in the wild areas. They have debated the difference between beauty and ugliness, for thousands of years, with no conclusion.

Their artists are obsessed with mortality. "What is the meaning of all song?" one poet asks. And then he answers his own question, "... that this, too, must pass away." This situation, this house, this love relationship, this poem, this town, this mountain, this island, this galaxy — this, too, must pass away. He knows it, and he doesn't like it. And it's not because of his loyalty to his town or his galaxy — it's because of his ego, his love of himself, as one tiny instance of humanity. This "I" must also pass away.

They are universal in declaring that ashes, bones and excrement are ugly. "How so?" we could ask. I have asked it more than once. "How are these bones not beautiful? Are they not sure signs of life?"

"Life that is past, gone, ended."

"Ended?" I asked. "It is never ended." Then I wondered if I wasn't verging on interfering. Don't they know *that?*

The ego of the one I was talking with prevailed. "I will die. You will die. My wife has died already. If I marry another, she will die, or I will." He seemed to be wallowing in misery, a kind of misery caused by the very basic facts of existence. Nothing lasts forever. But it was the ego he was fretting about, that was making him fret.

Their mortality and their egotism make them irrational. The more they think about death, the more it troubles them, usually. A few find a kind of comfort in thinking it all the way through, but they are dismissed as "morbid." Ego is always in the way. They are more loyal to themselves, their little fragile fleeting selves, than to the species as a whole, or what some of them call the Biosphere and I have called the Web of Life. They are more attached to ego, which is a mental invention and not really there at all, than to Reason itself, or Reasonableness.

Whenever an individual stumbles into rational thinking, we are encouraged. But as we watch, his ego goes to work and pretty soon he's indulging in irrational behavior, acting as if the reasonable insights he has come across do not apply to *him*. Every one of them thinks his ego is an exception to whatever rules his fragile little rational ability reveals.

Among the human species, individuals do better than groups, as far as rational behavior is concerned. Young ones, who are fairly clear-headed on their own, turn into needlessly nasty and belligerent specimens when grouped together in a schoolyard. Adults in groups can become a mindless, self-destructive mob with very little provocation. Trained adults can become robot-murderers, totally lacking in any sense even of self-preservation, let alone any sense of kinship or responsibility for those they are killing. Why anyone would want to train them into such behavior, or why they would consent to receiving the training which turns them into destructive mechanical devices under someone else's control, is something of a puzzle to us. Their largest groups, called nations, are totally irrational in behavior, and that fact constitutes a huge threat to the survival of the species.

◊   ◊   ◊

The species as a whole seems to be asleep, or sedated. The "leaders" are the least intelligent ones. Here and there remarkable individuals turn up, but they have no influence on developments. I became closely acquainted with one, named Robert, and he told me, "I am the keeper of fragile things." When I asked him what things, he replied, "Memory. Trust. Good will. Truth. Beauty." He was a poet and a painter of pictures, living very poorly, because those fragile things he was preserving are valued so *little* by the rest of his species.

Robert is a very unusual individual — they do appear from time to time, usually with little or no awareness of each other. Lonely specimens, they are, often artists of one kind or another. This one asked me, "How can a person be so at odds with his own culture?" He meant the larger group and the group's ideas, and the group's most influential teachers, and the group's most honored story-tellers. He felt that he was required, by his own understanding of the facts and his own best hopes for his own species, to oppose what was being said and done and proposed and approved and applauded in his group, which he called his culture. I asked him how he handled such alienation. What was he hoping to be able to do?

"I paint my pictures and tell my stories in an attempt to hold up what feel to me like universal values, or what *ought* to be universal values but obviously aren't in this dying culture. I'm trying to alter, a little anyway, the values, the beliefs, and even someday the customs and traditions of this culture."

"Sounds like quite a big job," I said.

"Yes. The only chance of success is to get into the story-telling business somehow — and offer a different set of heroes and heroines, and even a different set of problems that require solving."

"But at best that can have only a tiny effect," I suggested. "Stories are a dime a dozen, so to speak."

"Yes, but not *good* ones!"

"I have noticed that your culture, as you call it, prefers not to notice good stories. They prefer violence and conquest and slaughter and horror."

"I know. It's probably hopeless." He went on to discuss how an individual artist inherits all his tools from the very culture he feels so out of joint with. The axiomatic beliefs, what's been done before, what's comprehensible, the language itself — all that ties him to the culture he's fighting. He seemed to understand his situation quite well, but I did not think it likely that was going to effect much of a shift in values.

He proposed a specific example, and seemed to think his stories could make some kind of difference. "Here's a value I'd like to change," he said. "The value put on thermonuclear weapons as a means of defense. There's little question that my logic is better, and my 'values' are more basic and more all-inclusive. My stories illustrate my view of it. Here's one in which two children are exploring the causes of cancer. They confront, in ways that the adults generally refuse to do, the fact that *one* of the causes of cancer is man-made nuclear radiation. But this culture will not let my stories be told, on any scale wider than my personal conversations with people."

"You think your stories could change people's minds?" I asked.

"Well, I admit that telling and dramatizing my stories on every TV set in the country would have less effect, probably, than a serious nuclear accident. But then maybe not. We are actually in the midst of a series of nuclear accidents right now, and the people remain unconcerned. The leukemia rate right now, in the vicinity of those faulty facilities, is known to be up, up a *lot,* and no one, except those directly involved, seems to care much. Could these stories wake up some people? I guess I have to believe that it is worth the effort to try."

I wondered if his persistence was rational. Logic seems to be on the side of those who have lost hope, or never mustered enough concern to care at all. He went on.

"A nuclear war might do it." I realized he meant it might wake people up. "But, of course, a nuclear war would probably conclude the culture altogether. I think that would be too bad, a real crime and a shame. Alienated as I am, I only want to change my culture a little. I don't want it destroyed. It is badly flawed, for example in its illogical love affair with nuclear weapons, but I'd still like to help preserve it from its own tendency to self-destruct. I'm at odds, really, with only a part of it, the suicidal part."

I was *not* encouraged by our discussion, even though I was impressed deeply by *his* intelligence and courage and good will.

His words were logical. His thoughts were rational. But, once again, his actions looked a little crazy, and his own culture put that same evaluation on him. He was just another mad artist.

◇ ◇ ◇

We met another human who is perfectly aware of the danger their species is in, a friend of Robert, named Thomas. He is an amateur scholar, not connected to any of the universities which license professional scholars, but he is very thorough in his methods and his conclusions qualify as eminently rational.

He has a list of eighteen problems that confront humanity as a species, any one of which portends very serious difficulties and unpleasantness for the near future. His eighteenth problem is the human disinclination to take effective and practical steps to solve any of the previously-named problems. He believes, and it is patently obvious, that all of these eighteen threats to humanity, taken together, spell doom and extinction for his species.

Other observers of the human scene can quibble with his list of eighteen. Some of them could be listed as sub-sets of others. "Resource depletion" could take in "food depletion and famine," "ruination of topsoil," "depletion of forests," "depletion of oil." "Pollution" could encompass several kinds: "nuclear waste," "atmospheric pollution and acid rain," "ocean pollution," "fresh water pollution." Both "resource depletion" and "pollution" could be a subset of "overpopulation," which Thomas lists first and regards correctly as the all-pervasive problem. His list includes "global warming," "ozone layer depletion," "propensity of humans toward violence and war," and "obsession of humans with religion." His list could use some re-organization.

Thomas is another example of rational thought which is not followed up with rational behavior. "This is a species that loves to kill," he states. "It loves to kill, and exterminate, other species, and it loves to kill members of its own species." He says this in connection with one of his listed problems — "The Inclination toward Warfare and Violence." But as Thomas tells it, the same irrational violence becomes perceptible in *him,* in his voice, in the look on his face. "This species loves to kill," he growls, and we can see that love of killing, in him. He looks like he could kill somebody himself, on the spot.

His overall mood verges on irrationality. It is called despair. He and Robert are friends, and Thomas has disparaged, in my presence, the efforts of Robert to try to change things in some small way. "It is hopeless. Humanity is self-destructing. Humanity will soon be extinct." It demoralizes Robert even further, to have all this mass of irrefutable logic thrown at him to prove that his efforts to resist the trend, to try to wake people up, to try to say a word for decency and compassion and good sense, are all misguided and futile. It is irrational to assume that despair is "logical." Despair is one of the motivations for doing nothing to head off extinction. The despairing person is part of the threat, part of the problem.

His despair poisons Thomas's personal life, driving away friends, driving away those few who understand his eighteen reasons but haven't given up on trying to do something about them. Those people are rational enough to realize that they need not wallow in that kind of discouragement.

◇   ◇   ◇

Our tentative conclusion, after almost fifty orbits of observation, remains "pre-rational." That refers to both humans and dolphins. The latter haven't learned to apply reason to defense. The former have learned to apply reason to weaponry, but cannot muster the rationality to stop fighting one another. The mammoths and sabre-toothed tigers that the defense used to be aimed at have been extinct for thousands of years. The possibility that the humans will cause themselves to be extinct does not yet affect their behavior in any significant way. The humans have the rational concept of "endangered species," but do not think the phrase applies to themselves.

"Pre-rational, and in trouble."

◇   ◇   ◇

Job Two

"Nothing works," she said.

"Not without electricity," he agreed.

"So what do we do?"

He took a deep breath. "I saved an old-fashioned hand-pump, like my great-grandmother had in her back yard. I'll hook it up right away. Thank God, we have a good well. Maybe I'll get a windmill rigged up later. The monopoly is defunct, for good, like everything else, but we'll get along somehow."

"Why should we?" she asked.

"We'll plant a bigger garden, eat less, gather firewood at the river."

"With no vehicle?"

"The truck's fine, but there's no gas, and there won't be any. I'll use the wheelbarrow. The exercise will do us good."

She glared at him. "Good! You're crazy! Everything's destroyed. There's no one left alive but us. Why work as hard as you're imagining? Why go on? Why the hell go on living?"

"We gotta."

"We do *not* gotta. You tell me why."

"Because we're still here."

"Big deal. Another lonely night with you, and no T.V. Not even radio."

"There's no electricity, and no one's broadcasting anyway. I must admit I enjoy the silence."

◊   ◊   ◊

"You never stop while the sun is up. You work, like you never did before. Spading, wheelbarrowing all kinds of crap. Shoveling that stupid compost. Hauling firewood here, cutting it up. Work, work, work, all the day long. Why?"

110

"We hafta," he said.

"We do *not* hafta," she replied. "It's stupid. It's idiotic. Who says we hafta? Hafta do what?"

"Go on living."

"I don't want to go on living. I want to die. Curse God and die!"

"Why are you so angry?" he asked. "Let's make the best of it. We're still here, even if no one else is. We're healthy, which is pretty amazing. The work is not difficult."

"Not? You're exhausted all the time!"

"I mean it's not complicated. I don't have to wonder what to do. I just have to do it, so I do it. I tire myself. I sleep all night, which I didn't use to do. I get up rested. I work some more. It's not a bad life."

"It's a stupid life. Nothing but work."

"You're too angry to sense the satisfaction I'm finding. Why is that?"

She thought a moment. "Back when we could have saved things, you thought I was stupid. I agitated, wrote letters, made phone calls, marched, picketed, got arrested for protesting. You made fun of us. You didn't believe anyone should ever protest anything. You made money —what good does all your money do us now!" she shrieked. "You made piles of worthless money, you played golf, you watched football, you got drunk!"

"I'm sorry," he said, very quietly. "So *that's* why you're so mad."

"You laughed at us, and said it did no good to protest what was going on, that it wasn't as bad as we made out. You believed those liars who sold the beer and the football games and the wars and the plutonium. You laughed!"

"I was wrong."

"Wrong! That's hardly the word for it! Now there's nothing left. And you act almost glad! You *are* nuts! You never fought it at all, when there was still time. You thought protest was un-American. You paid your taxes!"

"I know. I was wrong. I'm sorry. You were right and I was

wrong. Just like the Vietnam War earlier. You were right. The war was wrong, and I was wrong not to say so. But that's all gone now. And we must go on."

"Why? Humanity is gone!" she said.

"Humanity deserved what it got. The miracle is that we're still alive, that humanity evidently has not yet been entirely extincted."

"We'll be dead shortly, no matter how hard you work. So when we're gone, humanity will then be extinct. Humanity isn't worth keeping alive. The King of Brobdignag was right."

"Who?"

"'I cannot but conclude the bulk of your natives to be the most pernicious race of little odious vermin that nature ever suffered to crawl upon the surface of the earth!'"

"Oh. Something you read. I notice that you read, while I work," he said.

"Humanity isn't worth it."

"Maybe we can start over." He looked at her face directly.

"Start over? Not me. Don't grin at me. I'm sixty-eight years old! I wouldn't dream of it. Not for a minute. Forget those funny ideas. Not me. Curse God and die."

"It *is* foolish, I admit," he said. "But we gotta go on."

"No, we don't."

"Life must go on. Life *will* go on."

"It's partly your fault."

"Between us two we can say that it's entirely my fault. But we don't quit now. We don't blame God and quit. Man-made problems are gone. So now we go to work on the more elemental problems, like water, food and warmth. The Whole Thing is all right."

"You're full of crap. It is *not* all right. Any idiot can tell by looking that it is not all right."

"We may have to move."

"Move? To where?"

"Somewhere near flowing fresh water. Somewhere warmer, where I can garden year round. Near the ocean, maybe."

"That's hundreds of miles. On foot."

"We can take it easy."

"I'm not going anywhere."

"Well, we won't fight. We'll share. We'll talk. We'll agree, before we do anything. Survivors will be sharers."

"There aren't any survivors!" she yelled.

"We're still here," he said.

"We won't be for long. Your cheerfulness, given your prospects and your responsibility for what's happened, make me sick. I still say, curse God and die."

"It does no good to blame God for this. We'll work while we can, and die when we must."

◇ ◇ ◇

If I Should Die

When a middle-aged man takes his body, and his spouse's, over to a lawyer's office, and talks at some length about his last will and testament, his thoughts and memories receive a special little jab.

Until now I never thought the little I've accumulated would be worth making a will about. But little as it is, I want the kids to have it, evenly divided among them. It would be a crying shame, really, if the politicians ended up with it.

But the process infects a body's thinking. Who will die first? Won't that be a mess! When one of us dies, I'm going to visit India. Maybe I should check out this pain in my leg, and this itching spot on the back of my hand. And I *will* have to return to the dentist again soon. Am I falling apart, or is it just my imagination? Or is it this will business?

Then I remember something — what a strange thing to pop into one's mind, and so vivid, too! I'm ten years old, and my little sisters are saying their prayers, on a bright northern summer evening, at the plump knees of our mother, who is in her underwear. It is the girls' bedtime, and then some, but they are not sleepy. Mom is tired, bone-weary, utterly fatigued by the heat and the humidity and a hard day at the factory. The girls are spry and alert. Rebecca watches, while Rachel prays.

"Now-I-lay-me down-to-sleep —
I-pray-the-Lord my-soul-to-keep —"

Mom has her head tilted back and her eyes closed. Rachel forgets the third line. Mom waits, weighted down with weariness. Rachel cannot continue. Her little feet squirm beneath her, sticking out from her little nightie. Rebecca watches, wide-eyed. Rachel is thinking of something else, looking at a bright little toy she has in her little fist.

At last Mom prompts, very weary, very disgusted, "If I should die —" Rachel is paying no attention at all. Rebecca waits in silence, watching, thinking — but no one knows what Rebecca is thinking. "If I should die —" growls Mom again, smacking Rachel lightly on the rump.

"Oh! —
    If-I-should-die before-I-wake —
    I-pray-the-Lord my-soul-to-take."

Rachel rattles through the rest of the God-blesses and the make-me-a-good-girl, all on automatic.

I remember that scene, all in an instant. My mind is stuck on, "If I should die." Is there any "if" to it? Oh, I understand, the "if" is that I may not die this very night, before I wake. But what a thing to teach to little kids!

I do not now believe that the words meant much, then. To me they certainly did not. I suppose I could ask my sisters. I cannot ask my mother. She *has* died, at her task, not in bed. What I remember of the praying is that almost meaningless assortment of phrases, memorized, and required to be recalled as each day ended. I was often not sleepy either, at the prescribed time. My mind was certainly not on the meaning of, *"If I should die —"*

The words mean more now. If I should die before I wake, I'd better get the damn will ready. And I'd better get at whatever it is that I want to do, and have accomplished, before then. In my case, that feels like quite a lot. I really do suspect that I'll run out of time, before I run out of things I want to do and see and learn and understand.

If I should die, I'd better tell those I love that that's the case, and behave accordingly.

And now the word "should" catches my eye. I know it's antiquated grammar, tied to the word "if," not to things like obligation or cosmic justice. But who thinks he should die? Not me. And that probably won't prevent it, either. I'm convinced we'd all better get at the living, now, while we can.

◇   ◇   ◇

Would This Help?

Marshall was an old man, recently widowed after a good marriage of many years. He felt weary, deep in his bones. The doctor had cut tiny patches of cancer from the skin of the back of each hand, and gave ominous warnings about the danger that it could quickly "go deep." He suffered some pain and frustration from a partial hernia.

Marshall's mind was alert. His memory was excellent, both long term and short term. He spent much of his time reading and arranging his written memories and observations in three-ring notebooks. He wrote some poetry. He never sent any of his writings out for publication, not believing that anyone else would be interested in any of it.

His reading and his memories and his observations made him sick at heart. He lamented the state of the world, the growth of seemingly insoluble problems and the fact that most of those difficulties were caused by his own species. He was often angered by the refusal of persons in positions of power even to recognize that there are such problems as hunger, starvation, poisoned water supplies, homelessness, radioactive contamination, acid rain and global warming. "They'd rather study it than do anything about it," he noted.

Marshall wanted to die. He wondered about all the stories he found that indicated that persons could decide to die and then do it, as if turning off a switch inside there somewhere. The ones who could do so seemed to be those who had found a kind of inner peace, or acceptance of the inevitable. They were really finished living, and so could decide to die, and then do so, without any kind of external weapon.

Marshall went back over his life in his mind, and decided that

116

he had had a good full life, that he had no real personal complaint about how it had all turned out. "Win some, lose some, some days it rains." But all in all, his life was all right, and worth the trouble. But now it was over, or almost.

Marshall decided, however, that he didn't want to die "for nothing." He didn't want to die "in vain," as so many had. He recalled that the phrase "died in vain," referred to warriors. It came from Lincoln's *Gettysburg Address,* in which he was dedicating a military cemetery. A song came to mind:
"As he died to make men holy,
Let us die to make men free."
The same war, he recalled, and the same elevation of messy military casualties to pious-sounding heights of glory. Marshall decided that all that was crap.

But he still didn't feel like merely exiting the scene. He wanted to do something in the dying, if it was possible. "You die anyway," he recalled, after all the effort and expense of trying not to. But he wasn't satisfied with just making room, merely getting out of the way. He wanted to effect something, in his dying.

Marshall thought of Kamikaze warriors, fighting for Japan in World War II. In his youth "Kamikaze" meant crazy, fanatical, non-quite-human, enemies of freedom and goodness. He had learned to put all that into perspective, and found himself trying to imagine the state of mind of those warriors who were ready to sacrifice themselves.

He recalled the Buddhist monks who burned themselves in Saigon in the middle of the war there. Their courage and their spirit demoralized the invaders and contributed to their final defeat and ouster, he thought. The dying of the monks *did* accomplish something — it overcame, finally, an invading force.

It would take some doing, on the inside. Fear would have to be overcome. Ego would have to be left behind. Not a bad idea, but no emperor would be worth it, for him. Marshall didn't believe in emperors, or even governments. But one could do this for humanity, maybe. One could do this for the world, yes.

Marshall decided to set fire to himself in public. The Imperial President was coming to the city in a few weeks, to speak at a fund-raising rally for Congress-persons of his party.

Marshall sought an accomplice. Since his wife's death he hadn't done much visiting. He felt awkward, seeking serious human contact again. Conversations felt disjointed and superficial, and reminded him of television commercials. People did not want to get serious and stay serious. He found he couldn't bring his proposal up at all. People refused to talk about age, dying, world problems or the future of humanity.

Marshall became discouraged and was tempted to go back to the idea of simply exiting quietly and privately, and let it go at that. Then a young friend whom he hadn't seen in several years came visiting, and he *did* want to talk about important things. So Marshall finally broached his subject. "If I bought the gasoline, and dumped it on myself and my protest sign, would you toss a match?"

"No!" answered his young friend, instantly and with vehement certainty. "I would not. It would be wrong, and it wouldn't do any good."

Marshall was on his own after all, in his decision to try to effect something with his dying. He thought of several Kamikaze murder/suicide schemes, in which both he and the Imperial President ended up dead, and decided he didn't want to commit murder, not even of a bloody-handed murderer, believing that it would detract from the long-range effect of what he would want his death to say or accomplish. No, the Buddhists knew what to do, and did it right.

Marshall made a sign, which said simply:

Our Taxes Murder Innocent People.

As he painted the letters, he thought of death squads in Central America and leukemia victims who lived near nuclear bomb factories. He filled two large thermos bottles with gasoline.

On the day of the visit of the Imperial President, he went to the Convention Center early in the morning, with a blanket and a picnic basket which contained his thermos bottles. He waited several hours, seated on the blanket holding his sign. A crowd gathered, as the time drew near for the arrival of the Imperial President. Marshall could hear the sirens of the police escort, getting louder. Then he heard harsh gruff voices barking, "Make way! Stand back!" He opened the first thermos bottle and poured gasoline on his head, down his back, down his arms. He opened the second and poured it on his chest and into his lap. Persons nearby exclaimed, "I smell gas! What's going on?"

The people standing around Marshall's blanket stepped back to make way for the shoving secret service agents. "Stand back!" Marshall struck a wooden match. The gasoline ignited with a "whoosh!" Marshall heard several people scream. He stared past the government agents into the face of the Imperial President. He looked deep into those eyes, seeking some connection. He was not sure that he established any. As the agents hurried the shaken Imperial President away, Marshall fainted and toppled over onto his side.

◇   ◇   ◇

Vermin

One

Above the Baseboard of the Kitchen hung the large metal grating of the air-conditioner vent. A voice came echoing down from above, "Anybody down there?" After a pause, a scratching on metal. "Anybody home?" Then a flapping of something soft but solid on metal, up inside the vent. "Hey! Answer me!"

A male rat popped his head up from a huge drawer, partly open, that ran along one side wall. He turned back and spoke down into the drawer, quietly but excited. "Somebody's coming! Somebody's here!"

"Nobody home?" called the voice up inside the vent. A large black male crow dropped to the floor and paced behind the metal grating. "Yoo-hoo!" he yodeled, louder.

The rat spoke down into the drawer, "I'll go look." He climbed out and dropped to the floor.

"Hey! Over here!" called the crow.

The rat trotted to the air vent. "Hello! Who are you?"

"Help get us out of here," ordered the crow.

"How?" asked the rat.

The crow kicked the grating. "Get this thing loose." He grabbed the grating and rattled it.

The rat ran to the open toe of a huge worn-out workingman's shoe that lay on the floor nearby and called in. "Aristo! C'mon out a minute. Someone's here." He ran back to the vent.

A male cockroach stuck his head out of the shoe's torn toe.

"C'mon," said the crow. "Get this thing open."

A gorgeous female rat appeared at the upper edge of the open drawer. "What's the matter, Arnold?" she called to her mate. "Is it worth disturbing us?"

The male rat turned to look up at her. "It'll just take a minute, Sweetheart. We gotta get this guy outa here." He rattled the vent.

Aristo came from the shoe and shook the vent with Arnold. A female cockroach appeared at the toe of the shoe.

"C'mon, you guys," growled the crow.

"How do we know it can be trusted?" barked the female cockroach. "And how many of them are there?"

"One, Arbutus," said Arnold.

"Two," said the crow.

"And *what* are they?" continued Arbutus. "And are they contaminated?"

"I just hope it's not a prolonged interruption," pouted the female rat.

"And I hope they aren't planning to *eat* here," growled Arbutus from the toe of the shoe.

"There's only one of 'em," said Arnold.

Aristo approached their problem scientifically. "I think if we all worked together — you and I pull," he said to Arnold. "And you push at the same time," he suggested to the crow. "On three. Ready?"

"Yeah," said the crow. "Let's get it off."

"One!" yelled Aristo. "Two! *Three!*" They all strained and the vent moved a little. After several one-two-threes and quite a bit of "C'mon" and "Let's-do-it" they pulled the grating away from the wall.

The crow hopped out. "What a struggle!" he gasped, shaking his iridescent feathers.

"Yes," said Arnold the rat. "You're welcome."

"It is not!" barked Arbutus from the toe of the shoe.

Arnold turned to her and said, "I mean he's thankful we got him out, and so I'm saying, 'You're welcome.'"

"He never said he was thankful," Arbutus growled. "And don't say some newcomer's welcome, when he's not. And he's not. I believe it's a bird. An insectivorous bird, at that." She backed further into the shoe.

Arnold turned to the crow. "How'd you get in there?"

"At the roof," he answered. "Through the weather machine. How else can a body get into their houses?"

"See any of 'em?" Arnold asked.

"Nope," the crow answered. "They're gone."

"All of 'em?" asked Aristo the cockroach.

"They were absurd, anyway," stated the crow flatly.

"Absurd?" yelped Arnold. "How can you say that? They built our world." He waved his hands around the Kitchen. "Changed our lives completely."

"And now you say they're gone," Aristo said.

"Destroyed themselves," said the crow. "They were absurd."

Another crow, a female, dropped down the metal duct work, with great flapping and scratching and squealing. Arnold helped her out the vent opening. "So there *are* two of you," he said.

"Gentlemen and Ladies," announced the male crow. "Allow me to present my wife, Arlene. She's not well. My name is Ariel." He addressed Arnold directly. "And you are —"

"Arnold. My wife's name is Ardent," he added, nudging the female rat who had climbed out of the drawer.

Ardent snuggled suggestively against her husband. "Yes. I'm Ardent."

Ariel stared at the pair of rats a moment and then turned to the cockroach. "And you are —"

"My name is Aristo. My wife is Arbutus. She is shy." Arbutus had backed still further into the shoe.

"I am not," she growled, re-appearing at the toe of the shoe. "I'm suspicious."

Arnold spoke to Ariel. "You say your wife is sick?" Arlene sat drooped and sad-looking on the floor.

"Yes," said Ariel. "She's in bad shape."

"What are the main symptoms?" asked Aristo.

Arbutus spoke from the shoe. "She droops a lot. I can see that from here. And when a bird droops, it's in trouble."

Ariel answered Aristo. "Listlessness, with sudden intermittent fits of manic craziness." Aristo examined Arlene's eyes and throat. "Can you help her?" Ariel asked.

"We have no food," growled Arbutus.

"I'll get her a drink of water," said Arnold, running off excitedly.

"No food!" exclaimed Ariel.

"None to spare," said Arbutus.

"Oh, but you *do* have some!" barked Ariel belligerently.

Arnold returned with a glass of water. "Here," he said to Arlene. "Drink this. You'll feel better."

"You're not giving away water we're gonna need, I hope," Arbutus said nastily to Arnold.

"There's plenty of water," Arnold said, as Arlene drank it down.

When she finished, Arlene asked her husband, "Are they under the influence?"

"I don't think so," he replied. "And stop that silliness."

Arnold spoke to the pair of crows. "So, you two came in through the weather machine."

"And you think they were absurd," Aristo added.

"I sure do," affirmed Ariel.

"Well, give ten reasons," said Arnold.

"Not so many," Arbutus objected. "They'll stay too long."

Ardent rubbed herself against Arnold, not exactly coyly. "Yes, Darling. Not so many. We were busy. Remember?"

"I could give you twenty reasons," said Ariel. "And the first is — they had weather machines."

Aristo rubbed his hands together. "Let's discuss it."

"*They* discussed everything!" exclaimed Arlene, suddenly. "And look what happened to them!" She coughed and retched. The other five all froze and then turned slowly and stared at her a long time.

Arnold broke the tension, asking Ariel, "What about weather machines?"

"Utterly absurd," said the crow. "A machine to make it cooler in the summer. Right? Matched by another machine to make it warmer in the winter."

"What's absurd about that?" asked Arnold.

"They moved out of caves, which are naturally cool in summer and easy to warm in winter —"

"And, oh, so deliciously filthy!" added Ardent.

"— into buildings of concrete and glass," continued Ariel. "Almost impossible to warm *or* cool."

"Or get into," Ardent added further.

"But they made *us* comfortable, too," argued Arnold. "Warmer in winter, for instance."

"They weren't even comfortable themselves!" crowed Ariel.

Arlene quoted one. "'Take your sweater, Darling. It's July, and your office will be freezing.'"

Ardent quoted another. "'Yes, Mama. Thanks for reminding me.'"

Arbutus quoted another. "'Don't forget your Underarm Dry, Darling. It's cold out, so your office will be sweltering.'"

Ardent again. "'Yes, Mama. I just hope the perspiration doesn't stain my dress.'"

"Hotter inside in winter than they can stand it in the summer," said Ariel. "And so cold inside in summer, they were *sick* all the time. Coughing and sneezing all over one another, spreading misery everywhere —" Arlene coughed and gagged at length.

"They did have weak respiratory systems," Aristo noted.

"Absurd, they were," insisted Ariel. He addressed the rats. "They didn't have nice fur insulation, thick or thin as the season would indicate, like you guys." He turned to the cockroaches. "They didn't breathe through holes in their tummies, and ignore temperature, like you guys." He spoke to his wife. "And they didn't fly away to Brownsville, or Banff, depending — like us."

"I'm convinced, Ariel," said Arlene. "And besides, they spent most of their time under the influence."

"Influence of what?" asked Arnold.

"Ignore her," said Ariel. "She's not well. And sometimes —" He stopped, and turned that imaginary crank beside the left side of his head.

◇ ◇ ◇

"So, you think the weather machine business proves they were absurd?" Aristo said to world-traveler Ariel.

"Too cold in summer and too stinking hot in winter," the crow re-affirmed. "And they cost oil to run. That started all the fighting over the oil — surely you all know the story — and that led directly to the end."

"The end. The end," chanted Arlene.

"'Unplug the damn weather machine!'" yelled Ariel, imitating someone. "'Let 'em sweat. Let 'em bundle up.'" He returned to his normal voice. "But, no."

"Well, I must say —"

Arlene interrupted Arnold. "He proved it."

"I'm thinking a thing," said Aristo philosophically. "The heat that warms us comes from the sun, right? The heat from the burning oil came originally from the sun, too. Right?"

"Yeah. So what?" asked Ariel.

"Do you know what percentage of the sun's rays reach the earth?"

"I'm sure I don't," admitted Arnold, but he was interested.

"No one knows such a thing," said Ariel. "And who cares? You sound as absurd as they were."

"Oh, no," said Aristo. "Some of them did ask questions like that, and they *weren't* absurd."

"Their Wise Guys should have asked more important questions," growled Arbutus. "About more relevant matters."

"Do you know the percentage, Aristo?" asked Ardent.

"Well, let's figure it out together," he replied. Then he turned to his wife. "And it *is* relevant. We think we're so important. Just like most of them did. You're gonna be surprised."

"Are you under the influence?" Arlene asked him.

Aristo was engrossed in his problem. "Solid geometry. The earth's orbit is the circumference of an imaginary sphere. The area of the surface of that sphere equals the total amount of the sun's rays sent out at any moment. The area of the great circle of the earth is the total amount of sun's rays reaching earth at any moment. Just compare your two numbers!" He mumbled figures and formulas aloud to himself as the others shook their heads at him. "Four pie are squared. Are equals ninety-three million. Hmm. Hmm. Pie are squared. Are equals four thousand."

"He's absurd," stated Ariel. "One crazy cockroach."

"Oh, no," protested Arnold. "He's very smart."

"He's a philosopher," said Ardent.

"He's under the influence," repeated Arlene.

"He's hard to live with at times," admitted Arbutus.

"The whole question is absurd," said Ariel.

"Here it is," announced Aristo. "Total rays reaching earth equals five times ten to the seventh. And total rays sent out equals one times ten to the seventeenth. Rounding things off. So that means —" He mumbled again, and the others resumed their comments.

"Stark raving absurd!" asserted Ariel.

"No. Very impressive," said Arnold.

"Under the influence!" insisted Arlene.

Aristo became excited. "For every ray of the sun that reaches the earth, two billion rays go off away from the sun in all other directions. That's important!"

"It is not!" contradicted Ariel.

"It *is!*" Aristo insisted. "And important to think about. I think they should have thought about it more than they did."

"They were absurd," muttered Ariel, turning away. Then he said to his wife, pointing at Aristo, "That one may indeed be under that influence of yours. Keep your eye on him."

"Let's hear another of your marvelous proofs," Arnold suggested to Ariel.

"Very well," he agreed. "They had throttles."

"Throttles!" exclaimed Aristo. "What are they?"

"A device invented to inflict cruel torture on half of them, especially in summer, except those in their over-chilled buildings. It worked in winter in the over-heated places. Totally absurd," Ariel stated.

"'Straighten your tie, Harold!'" cawed Arlene, imitating one of them.

"No useful result came of it," explained Ariel further. "Only trouble, fighting, gagging, gasping for air and general restriction of movement."

"'Where'd you find that grotesquely ugly tie, Marvin?'" asked Arbutus, quoting another.

"What was this device?" Aristo asked.

Ariel continued. "It started as a badge of rank, but slipped from garters on ankles to ruffles on lapels — to strings, cords, thongs, ribbons, bands, ropes, chains — around the *neck!*"

"'Tighten your noose, Harold,'" ordered Arlene.

"'But, Darling,'" protested Arnold. "'I'm not getting enough air as it is now.'"

"That faulty respiratory system, again," commented Aristo.

Arnold gasped and choked, imitating one of them. "'Air! More air! Why must I work with an unnecessarily restricted air supply?'"

"I think it must have been a symbolic penis," Aristo opined.

"One of their Wise Guys figured that out, finally," agreed Ariel.

"It's perfectly obvious," said Aristo.

"I can't imagine having any fun with it," Ardent said.

"Men only wore 'em," said Ariel. "Some complained, but it did no good."

Arnold imitated. "'How can they sit in this sweltering oil-burning heat with mammary glands hanging out all over the place, while I have to battle and gasp for an inadequate air supply?'"

"The only animal that wore clothes," Aristo added.

"Or needed to," Ardent added further.

"Or *thought* he needed to," added Arbutus still further.

"It was a badge of rank, for workers whose work entailed no work," explained Ariel.

Arnold imitated again. "'Why must we wear coats and ties,

Mr. Headmaster, Sir?'"

Ariel gave the answer. "'Because this is a school where you're learning how to get jobs that entail no work, and I insist you dress accordingly.' And they did what he said," he added.

Arlene became suddenly manic and alert. "The end was caused by men wearing throttles. They may or may not have been under the influence."

The others all froze, and then turned slowly and stared at her. After a pause, Aristo asked again, "What's this influence?"

"It's bad business," said Arlene. "They wore throttles around their necks, right? Well, let me tell you a story. And let it be a warning to you all."

"Talk about absurd," cracked Arbutus sharply.

"There's this guy," continued Arlene, oblivious to Arbutus' scorn. "Comes home from the overheated building. Takes his throttle off. Decides to take a bath, while under the influence. Draws hot water. He likes the feel of hot water on all his nerve endings. That stuff does weird things to you."

"You should know," sneered Arbutus.

"He's ready for a bath," continued Arlene. "Decides he needs a shave. And while shaving, he cuts a raised mole on his neck — right there where the throttle is tied on. He forgot to be careful. Cut it bad."

"'Ow! Ow!'" bawled Arnold, hopping around holding his neck. "'Help! Blood! My God! I slit my own throat!'"

"Well," continued Arlene, "you never heard such screaming and carrying on in all your life. Shrieking and bellowing and hollering, that he slit his own throat." Arnold continued to shriek and holler and run around the room.

"Well, you just said he *did!*" remarked Aristo.

"Hah!" croaked Arlene. "Yes. He sure did slice that old wart off — clean as a whistle."

"That's terrible," said Ardent with sympathy.

"And let that be a lesson to all of you!" concluded Arlene. She coughed and gasped and drooped.

Ardent turned to Arnold. "'Here, Honey. Let me wrap your

neck for you. If we wrap it nice and pretty and tight, it'll be all right.'"

"Wrapping it will fix it?" asked Aristo.

"That's what they thought," said Ariel. "They were really hung up on the wrappings. Absurd. They paid as much attention to the wrapping as they did to *what* they wrapped."

"'Shall I gift-wrap it for you, Sir?'" Arbutus asked, imitating one of them.

"'Yes, please,'" replied Arnold. "'And jazz it up. Extra bows, extra ribbons. You know. It's for my special Sweetie.'"

"What is it?" asked Aristo.

"'It doesn't matter,'" Arnold replied.

"'Oh, what a lovely gift!'" Ardent exclaimed, imitating one of them. "'Such a beautiful package!'"

"They spent as much on the wrappings as on the gift," explained Ariel.

Arlene addressed Arnold, imitating one of them. "'Sir, our cost analysis indicates that the can costs more than the stewed tomatoes that go into the can.'"

"'Thank you very much, Miss Glick,'" replied Arnold. "'That'll justify a ten percent price increase.'"

"They not only packaged everything they handled and sold and gave away to one another," said Ariel. "They even packaged themselves."

"'He looks so strange without his throttle,'" said Arlene, imitating.

"'I can hardly tell who is who in the hot tub,'" commented Ardent warmly.

Arnold leered at her. "Ha! There're only two kinds."

"'Halt!'" ordered Ariel, imitating one of them. "'You can't pass this gate. Lemme see your I.D.'"

"'Oh, Sir, I lost my wallet,'" replied Arnold. "'It was stolen.'"

"'Lemme see your I.D.'" Ariel insisted.

"'It's gone!'" Arnold lamented.

"'How can you prove you were born without a birth

certificate?'" Ariel asked.

"There he is!" Aristo commented, pointing. "He must have been born."

"That proves nothing at all," said Ariel. He turned back to Arnold, "'Where are your credentials?'"

"'I'm me!'" Arnold protested.

"'Not without identification you aren't,'" sneered Arbutus.

"'Prove that you *are* somebody,'" said Arlene.

"'Let me look at your resume,'" said Ariel. "'Where's your dossier?'"

"Why are you talking French all of a sudden?" asked Aristo.

"'I am me, standing, weeping, here before you,'" wailed Arnold.

"'Without I.D. and credentials, you are Nobody," insisted Ariel.

"'I can lift hundred-pound bales,'" offered Arnold.

"Very well," said Aristo. "Prove it. Lift this," he said, slapping a broom that was leaning against the wall.

"Oh, no," said Ariel to Aristo. "Nothing that logical. That's not how they did it." He turned to Arnold. "Try again."

"'I can lift hundred-pound bales,'" Arnold repeated.

"'You can?'" Ariel replied, imitating. "'Let's see your credentials. Do you have written proof? Signed by whom?'"

"'I do not *have* credentials,'" Arnold protested. "'Believe me. I am credible. I am me. I was born. I can do what I can do. I am who I am. I know what I know. I know who I am.'"

"'You are Nobody," said Arlene, coughing and gagging.

"'You lost your wrappings,'" added Ariel. "'And you're Nobody without 'em.'"

"That's absurd!" exclaimed Aristo.

"That's what I've been telling you," smirked Ariel.

"He proved it," concluded Arlene.

◇   ◇   ◇

"Throttles, wrappings. Anything more?" Aristo asked Ariel.

"Lots more, but why should I tell you?" the crow replied.

"Because we're curious," said Arnold. "We want to *know*."

"Well, we're hungry," said Ariel. "We want to *eat*."

"We'll have lunch soon,' Arnold said. "Tell us first."

"We will *not* have lunch soon," chirped Arbutus. "That is, *they* won't. We only have a little left. It has to last us —" She hesitated, and then glared at Arnold. "*You* decided that."

"We have some left," Arnold reported quietly. "We can share it."

"Why should we share with them?" squealed Arbutus. "Who are they?"

"We told you who we are," Ariel said. "Two lost crows. One sick. Both hungry."

"We'll share," Arnold assured him. "Tell us more of your proofs first."

Ariel looked from Arnold to Arbutus, then back to Arnold. "Can I trust you?" he asked.

"Sure," said Arnold. "We all *have* to trust each other."

"Tell us more," begged Aristo.

After a pause Ariel resumed. "Very well. They had freeways."

"What was free about 'em?" asked Ardent.

"They cost a million dollars a mile, before that last fatal inflation before the end."

"Freeways prove they were absurd?" Aristo asked.

Arlene imitated one of them. "'You better get started, Harold. You might get stuck on the freeway and be late.'"

"Where were they all going?" Aristo asked.

"During what they called Rush Hour, they were going to do their daily task, or coming home from doing it."

"'Gotta get to work,'" muttered Arnold.

"'Gotta get home,'" murmured Ardent.

"Why not trade tasks?" asked Aristo. "And not go?" He hesitated and then asked further, "Or do a task where one is already?"

"Or live where the task is located?" suggested Arbutus.

"Build apartment houses where the plant parking lot is now," proposed Ardent.

"Don't be so logical," said Ariel. "They weren't." After a pause, he added, "And some of them were just milling around, anyway, not going anywhere."

"Rats do that when they're crazy," Arnold informed them.

"You should know," cracked Arlene.

"And they had wrecks," said Ariel.

"Because they were reckless," Arlene added.

"Figure *that* out," sneered Arbutus.

"They didn't reckon," Ariel explained. "They couldn't be warned. They didn't learn."

"Crows can learn from experience," said Arlene smugly.

"So can rats," added Ardent. "Experiments have proved —"

Arlene interrupted her to ask Aristo, "Can cockroaches learn from experience?"

"Cockroaches are paying attention," said Aristo proudly, "and learning — all the time!"

"Indeed," added Arbutus.

Arlene imitated someone. "'I don't have to reckon. I'm an exception. I can be reckless.'"

Ardent continued. "'And so can I. It's bad for other folks, but not for me. I'm an exception.'"

"That's stupid," said Arnold.

"That's absurd," said Ariel. "Which is what I was demonstrating."

"Someone told me once that many of them had a certain dream," reported Aristo.

"They all acted like they were dreaming," snorted Arlene.

"It was a common dream among them," Aristo said. "Maybe universal." He quoted. "'I dreamed I was driving backward on the freeway.'"

"'Watch where you're going!'" screamed Arbutus.

"Normally they drove forward," said Aristo. "Watching where they were going, with the illusion that they *knew* where they were going."

Arnold imitated one of them. "'Hey, Joe! Where *are* we? We been driving and driving.'"

"In a driving-backward dream," proceeded Aristo, "it was obvious that they didn't know where they were going."

"'Whoops!'" shrieked Arlene. "'Oh! Not so fast! Where have we been? Stay on the road! Is there a road?'"

"It's exciting. And it's scary," added Aristo. The three females shrieked together. "But, then, after all, it is usually safely gotten through. Everybody does end up somewhere."

"That's absurd," said Ariel when he realized Aristo was finished. "As absurd as they were."

Arlene became suddenly manic and alert. "I think that one," she said, pointing at Aristo, "is under the influence."

"He is not," retorted Arnold. "He's just smarter than most folks."

"Let me tell you about the fellow, driving on the freeway in heavy traffic, paying more attention to the throbbing on his radio than to the traffic, doesn't brake in time to avoid striking and running over a purse-snatcher, who was fleeing the scene of his crime, crossing on foot the freeway, purse in hand."

"Oh, good!" exclaimed Arbutus, rubbing· her antennae together with pleasure. "Good for him. So she got her purse back."

"She did. But the driver was sent to the pen for reckless driving. And let that be a lesson to all of you!" Arlene concluded, and coughed and gagged and drooped.

"What's the pen?" Ardent asked, after a moment.

"Some of them thought it was a place where bad-deed-doers learned to be penitent," explained Ariel.

"But it wasn't," said Arlene wearily. "And they didn't."

"It was really a kind of cage," said Ariel, rattling the loose vent grating. "This place is kinda like one, actually." He looked around. "How do we get outa here?"

"Out?" asked Arnold in genuine surprise. "Who wants out?"

"I do," stated Ariel. "I'm sick of this discussion."

"*They* discussed everything," Arlene reminded them.

"We were just getting started," said Aristo. "Why leave?"

"*We* never do," said Arnold.

"No," added Ardent. "We have beds and food and beds and water and beds and companionship."

"*We* don't," croaked Ariel. "Yet." He stared upward. "Is that a door?" he asked.

"It is," said Aristo.

"How do you open it?" Ariel demanded.

"I don't open it," Aristo replied. "Any one of several of *them* used to come and open it. But not lately."

"Maybe one of them will come again and open it," said Ardent. "Although why anyone would want to leave is a puzzle to me," she added.

Ariel returned to the air vent and stepped inside and looked up and all around. "None of *them* is coming," he said flatly.

Arlene staggered to the vent opening. "What are you looking for in here?" she asked her feathered mate.

"A way out," he answered, staring upward. "We'll never be able to fly in that tight place."

Arlene emerged, resigned. "No. We'll have to stay."

Ariel emerged and said, "Feels like a pen." He turned to Arnold, "You say there's no problem with the water supply?"

"No. Our — uh, host didn't trust the city chlorine department. Had fresh water piped in from the creek. Plenty of it. Not contaminated. We're lucky."

"Get my mate another drink," Ariel ordered brusquely.

"Sure," said Arnold and he scurried off.

Ariel spoke to Aristo. "What food do we have here?"

"*You* don't have any," Arbutus snapped nastily. "Unless you brought it with you."

Ariel turned to her and demanded, just as nastily, "I'm asking what food *you* have."

"Why should we tell you?" she demanded.

"We'll not fight over it," Ardent said.

Arnold returned and offered a glass of water to Arlene. She drank a little, and then handed the glass to Ariel.

Ariel repeated his question to Aristo. "What food do you have?"

"Corn," said Aristo.

Ariel took a long drink. "How much?"

"I don't know," said Aristo. "Arnold's in charge of it."

"He is," said Arbutus. "But I *should* be."

"We have some to share," Arnold stated. He spoke to Ariel. "Relax. We'll have lunch in a little while. Tell us about their bad-deed-doers."

Ariel studied Arnold's face a moment. "Very well," he said at last. "They weren't really trying to prevent bad deeds. Thieves who took millions and murderers who killed thousands never went to pens at all."

"But he was forced to quit it, at least," whimpered Arlene. "And he suffered plenty, really. Didn't he?" They all froze, and then turned slowly and stared at her. There was a long pause. She broke it finally, exclaiming, "Well, you can't put presidents and generals in the *pen!*"

Ariel proceeded. "They made no effective effort to prevent bad deeds, like burglary and rape. Persons who resisted bad-deed-doers got into trouble themselves. Citizens were advised not to fight to defend themselves."

"That does sound absurd," admitted Aristo. Arbutus knocked on the drawer with authority. Aristo went along with the charade. "'Yes, Sir. What can I do for you, Officer?'"

Arbutus imitated one of them. "'This gentleman says he broke into your house and you tied him up and hung him from the ceiling by the wrists without food or water for three days and then let him go.'"

Aristo played along. "'He's confessing to the bad-deed of breaking and entering? That's interesting. Shouldn't you handcuff him?'"

"'Is he the man?'" asked Arbutus.

"'He broke that window and entered my house. Yes.'"

"'Yes, I did,'" said Arnold. "'And then he tied me up and starved me!'"

"'What about that?'" Arbutus asked Aristo.

"'Are you going to believe a confessed felon?'" Aristo asked in turn.

"'Look at my wrists!'" Arnold cried.

"'How do you account for those rope burns?'" Arbutus asked Aristo.

"'I don't,'" Aristo replied. "'And I don't have to. He may be under some kind of influence that I don't know about.'" He smiled and nodded to Arlene, and then proceeded. "'Some people spoil their lungs, others their livers, others their noses. He may be a wrist person. What about the *admitted* breaking and entering?'"

"'You better come with me,'" Arbutus said to Arnold.

"But that's not what happened," Ariel concluded.

Arlene broke in, imitating someone. "'I have here my burglar-catching machine. Adapted from the Tasmanian devil-trap, the Annamese tiger-trap and Dinkenblinken's sausage machine. It wraps and packages what it catches. Enough cat-food can be produced —'"

"Cat-food!" exclaimed Ardent, interrupting.

"'With widespread use, the whales may be saved,'" Arlene continued.

"Don't be ridiculous," said Aristo. "What about the bad-deed-doer's rights?"

Ariel picked up on that. "*That* notion is what drove them deepest into absurdity. The bad-deed-doers had rights and their victims did not."

Ardent quoted someone. "'Do we have the right to life, liberty and the pursuit of happiness? Or do we have to let them break down our doors and windows, steal our things, rape and murder us?'"

"Accused bad-deed-doers have rights," asserted Aristo.

"Agreed," said Ariel. "But do bad-deed-doers in the act of committing bad-deeds have rights?"

Arbutus quoted someone. "'We citizens claim the right to defend ourselves. You won't need pens, if the citizens are allowed and encouraged to defend themselves, and if violent bad-deeds are thoroughly and effectively punished on the spot.

The citizen must be judge and jury and Lord High Executioner, on the spot. Retrain rapists, burglars, muggers, purse-snatchers and breakers-and-enterers, on the spot.'"

Ardent continued. "'All rights of bad-deed-doers are forfeit upon entering into the bad-deed.'"

"You can't do that," Aristo protested. "You can't kill burglars."

"'My invention here —'" began Arlene.

"It's against the law to kill burglars," insisted Aristo.

"Isn't it against the law to burgle?" asked Ardent.

"Yes, it is. But —" Aristo stalled.

Arlene proceeded. "'My machine here prevents burglary. There's no more efficient way to prevent burglary.'"

"The police are not trying to prevent it," said Aristo.

"'Well, *we* are," chirped Arbutus. "'The Associated Victims of Bad-deeds, Incorporated, is dedicated to the prevention and eradication of it.'"

"You want the death penalty for theft?" asked Aristo.

"'No,'" replied Arlene. "'We want restitution, four-fold, to the victims. And we want theft stopped. This machine will do it. We recommend its widespread use.'"

"'If it is used,'" chimed in Ardent, "'the day will come when it will be widely understood that to become a thief is to become dead. To steal is to commit, not a bad-deed, but suicide.'"

Arbutus continued. "'No amount of profit to be gained by theft is worth such a sure and certain prospect of self-extermination. It will become a seldom-used method of self-destruction, not a way of life for thousands.'"

Ardent proceeded. "'It will be approximately as dangerous as stepping out a twenty-story window. Don't do it. You might, by accident, survive a time or two, but don't count on it. The odds are against it. It's a form of suicide.'"

"Sounds logical to me," said Aristo.

"Yes," said Ariel. "But that's not how they handled it. What they did instead proves their absurdity."

"What did they do?" asked Aristo.

"They had lawyers. And everybody lost every case, to *them!*"

"They kept the world safe for bad-deed-doers," said Arbutus. "Until lately. We haven't seen any lately, good or bad."

Arlene became suddenly manic and alert. "Let me tell you about this guy, gets the notion that he's controlling, or causing, his own thoughts. I mean, that's weird! Anyone knows you don't *cause* your own thoughts. They just pop into your head."

"I cause some of *my* thoughts," stated Aristo.

"I can imagine," said Ariel. "But I think you're under their influence."

"He is not!" objected Arnold. "He's just smarter than anybody else —"

Arlene interrupted. "Anyway, this guy's thinking his thoughts, and he gets the further notion that his thoughts *cause* things to happen, even at a distance."

"Oh-oh," said Aristo.

"He suddenly gets the idea that there's a burglary going on at his house. And he thinks he's *causing* it, because he's thinking it."

"That's absurd," said Arnold.

"We been telling you that all along," Ariel reminded him.

"Decides he needs to go home," continued Arlene. "Quick. Race home, speeding in the car on the freeway. Hurry, hurry." She paused.

"Well?" asked Arbutus.

"Nothing," said Arlene. "No burglary. Everything's fine. Nobody home. TV in place. No trouble. All for nothing." She coughed and drooped.

After a moment Aristo murmured, "But he was on to something."

"*You'd* think so," said Ariel.

"Magic, maybe," continued Aristo. "The power of the mind."

"But he was wrong," said Arbutus.

"Yes," admitted Aristo. "Too bad."

"Too bad!" exclaimed Ardent. "Who wants her house robbed?"

"No," said Aristo sadly. "I don't mean that. I mean he could do it, but it scared him. He could make things happen, mentally, but he didn't want the responsibility. Most folks don't. We'd rather be told, or driven, or manipulated, or swept along — rather than be responsible for what happens."

"You're absurd," said Ariel.

"But we *are* responsible," continued Aristo quietly. "After all. Anyway, whatever we do. Or don't do." He mused a moment and then turned to Arlene. "Interesting story."

Arlene backed away from him. "You're weird. Really."

Ariel addressed Arnold. "When is lunch?"

"In a little while," Arnold replied. "Tell us more."

◇   ◇   ◇

"You're interested in them, aren't you?" Ariel asked Arnold.

"Yes," Arnold admitted.

"You even like them. Or liked them, I should say. They're all gone now."

"If so, that's too bad," said Arnold. "Tell us more."

"I'd rather talk about lunch," said Ariel.

"There won't be any lunch, for you," sneered Arbutus.

"Sure, there will," said Arnold. "We'll share. Right, Aristo?"

"The math is difficult," mused the philosophical cockroach. "I don't know exactly how much corn is left."

"Not enough," growled Arbutus.

"Whatever it is — divided by four..." Aristo mumbled to himself. "Divided by six..." He mumbled further. "Let's see. One-fourth, one-sixth." He looked at Arnold. "Each of us would have to reduce from twenty-five-ex to sixteen-and-two-thirds-ex." He addressed the crows. "And each of you would increase from zero to sixteen-and-two-thirds-ex."

"Your stupid mathematics!" Arbutus shouted at her mate. "Forget it. We have a little. We need it *all*. It's just too bad for them."

"You could eat and watch them *starve?*" Arnold asked her.

"And you think we *would?*" asked Ariel. "I mean, just lie

down and starve, watching you eat?" He climbed up on the drawer and looked in. Then he hopped down and jumped up on the shoe and stretched up toward the top. "Where do you keep it?" he demanded.

"We'll never tell," said Arbutus.

Arnold turned to his mate. "What do you think, Honey?"

"I say let's share it," pronounced Ardent grandly. "Share it all and be done with it. And die loving."

After a pause, Aristo said, "That's magnificent."

"It is not," said Arbutus flatly. "It's stupid."

"You don't want to share?" Ardent asked Arbutus.

"No," she replied. "I do not."

"Why not?" Ardent asked.

"I don't want to die," said Arbutus.

"Oh, you have to die," said Ardent. "Eventually. You're acting like too many of *them.*"

"I don't want to die *now,*" insisted Arbutus.

"Neither do I," said Ardent. "But that's not what's important. Not really. We all die sooner or later. So, will we die hating and fighting, or will we die loving? I say share it."

"Why should we?" shrieked Arbutus.

Ardent was very matter-of-fact. "You'll end up dying sooner, fighting over it. Like they did." She turned to Ariel. "Tell us more about them. We'll all eat together afterward."

Ariel stared into Ardent's face with something like reverence. "I will, if you want me to," he said softly.

"You were telling about their bad-deeds," she reminded him.

"So were you," he said quietly. He continued staring at Ardent for a moment, before he returned to his argument. He looked around at the others. "They didn't even really object to bad-deeds at all in the most glaring cases. Highly organized, nationally funded bad-deeds, I mean."

"Such as what?" asked Ardent.

"Such as war. They called it 'defense.' It was really arson, trespass and murder." Ariel glared hard at Arbutus.

"Yes," said Ardent. "War. And we don't need World War

Four in here."

"Assault, theft, kidnapping," continued Ariel. "But mostly arson and murder."

"You say they didn't object?" asked Aristo.

"They didn't. They voted for it. Paid for it. Encouraged it. Did it."

"Why?" asked Arnold. "What good did it do?"

"Good!" yelped Ardent. "Who said it did any good?"

"They wouldn't do it," said Arnold, "if they didn't believe it would do any good."

"They *did* believe that," said Ariel. "Some of them. But they were absurd, as I'm telling you. They believed that organized arson, assault, trespass and murder could do good. 'Defend their freedom,' they said."

"Even if they didn't have any," added Aristo.

"The ones around here claimed they had freedom," said Arnold.

"And over in China they did not," chimed in Arbutus. They all froze, and then turned slowly and stared at her. After a pause, she explained. "In China, someone decided whether you may or may not travel."

"'Lemme see your traveling pass,'" said Ardent, imitating someone.

"In China, someone decided what daily task you were going to do after your training was over," continued Arbutus.

"'Report at the shoe factory on Monday at seven,'" quoted Ardent again.

"Here it was decided by default," said Arbutus.

Arlene imitated someone. "'If you have the money, Sonny, and can afford to neglect your normal source of more money for a time, you may travel. If you don't have a source you can be away from for a while, you may not.'"

"But no one ever said that in so many words," explained Arbutus.

Arlene continued. "'If you can find a job, Johnny, take it and do it. If you can't find one here, look there. If you can't find a place to do what you've been trained to do, do something else.'"

"But no one ever told anyone that in so many words," said Arbutus. "No one openly said that. You had to figure it out."

"Having to figure it out," mused Arnold. "That's freedom."

"In either case, you had to do what you had to do. There someone told you. Here you had to figure it out," Arbutus repeated.

"That's what freedom *is*," said Arnold.

"Not everyone was enthused about it," said Aristo. "Not everyone wanted to go thousands of miles away to defend it."

"And," said Ariel, "large numbers of them, even where 'freedom' was abundant, were happy to forego exercising it by attaching themselves to bureaus and institutions which made their lives positively Chinese. Career military. Career clergy. Career organization. Jobs, jobs, jobs!"

"Someone told them," said Aristo. "They didn't have to figure it out."

"So," said Arnold, "freedom was a lot of trouble, and maybe not worth defending."

"But," said Ariel, "they were nevertheless persuaded to believe that it was, and they fought absurd wars over it."

"But sometimes they were defending their houses and their beds," said Ardent.

"They always said so," admitted Ariel. "Even ten thousand miles away."

"Sometimes they stood —" said Ardent, and then she quoted something. "'— between their loved homes and the war's desolation.'"

"Sometimes," said Ariel. "The absurdity was caused by empire."

"You know," said Aristo thoughtfully. "I've been pondering the optimum size of a nation."

"What is it?" asked Arnold.

"An area that gets entirely the same weather," defined Aristo.

"You are weird," Arlene said to him. "And surely under the influence."

"The U.S.A. was too big," continued Aristo. "The U.S.S.R. was far too big. China was too big. Great Britain redivided just before the end, you remember. And so did the Soviet Union."

"Name a country that is the correct size," said Ardent.

"Wales," answered Aristo. "Belgium. Rhode Island."

"'And here's today's weather report,'" quoted Arnold. "'Today it rained.'"

"All descriptions of weather in other places would be 'news from abroad,'" said Ardent.

"'Today was clear and sunny in Delaware,'" reported Arnold.

"The consequence would be a large number of countries, every one of which is far too small to afford a three hundred billion dollar annual war budget," explained Aristo. "Countries could hardly afford war at all."

"Yes," said Ariel. "The empires were absurd. Far too large. And with ten thousand miles of ocean also in the way, they could enforce their will only with weapons which meant the end of everything. It was all bluff from half a planet away."

Arnold imitated someone. "'They know we can't really effect anything so far away. But we hope they think we aren't bluffing. That is, we hope they think that we *are* ready to destroy life on this planet in order to avoid having to live without that oil.'"

"'We hope they think we're crazier than they are.'"

"You *are!*" said Arlene. "That is, *they were!*"

"The Empire is the bully on the corner," said Aristo.

Ariel proceeded. "Nineteen-year-olds, at first, and then everybody, had to pay with their lives for the unfortunate privilege of having been born in a country which happened to be the bully on the corner."

Arnold quoted somebody. "'There are things worth dying for.'"

"If someone wants to die for something," stated Arbutus flatly, "he has my permission to go do so. But count me out."

"Me, too," agreed Ardent. "I enjoy living too much."

"'No, not me,'" said Arnold, continuing his quotation. "'I

mean all of *you!*'"

Ariel spoke to him. "You're a couple of wars behind, General. You used to send nineteen-year-olds out to die, and then think up reasons why it was worth it for them to do so. But the end-of-the-world weapons changed all that."

Aristo spoke to Ariel. "You're convincing me. It was all absurd."

"The proof was that their women liked it," said Ariel.

"Liked it?" squeaked Ardent. "How could they like having their homes and beds destroyed?"

"I don't pretend to understand that part," Ariel admitted.

Arbutus quoted someone, screaming. "'I'm so ashamed. My own son! Refusing to register! It's disgraceful. Get out. Get lost. You're no son of mine. I didn't raise my son to be an unpatriotic coward!'"

"'Listen, Mom —'" said Arnold.

"'Don't "Mom" me! Get out! I hate you! I never want to see or hear anything of you ever again!'"

"It *is* absurd to hate your own offspring," said Aristo.

"They did it all the time," said Ariel. "And when they weren't fighting wars, they were playing war games."

"Games instead of war?" asked Ardent.

"Mock war," said Ariel. "When they weren't committing actual literal arson and murder, they were setting up boards and pieces of ivory and cards and computers in which they assaulted, captured, took, killed, destroyed, neutralized and defeated one another."

"Sounds a little better than the actual burning and killing," suggested Aristo.

"It may have been," admitted Ariel. "But it became absurd. The games had rules, and the wars didn't, really. But winning the games became as desperate as any war."

"'Winning is not the most important thing,'" quoted Arnold. "'It's the only damn thing.'"

"They involved their children in the process," said Ariel.

"Younger than the nineteen-year-olds?" asked Ardent.

"The nineteen-year-olds fought the real wars, but the war games included eight-year-olds, and also doddering ancients," explained Ariel.

"'Gotta win,'" chanted Arlene. "'Gotta win.'"

"'We gotta kick their butts,'" said Arnold.

"'Shall I attack the hearts?'" asked Ardent.

"'I'll murder her queen with my bishop,'" muttered Arbutus.

"'Gotta win," chanted Arnold. "'Gotta win.'"

"The thing went in a circle," explained Ariel. "They began to think of war as if it was a game, with winners and losers and prizes and penalties. They even talked of winning that last final all-destructive outburst of violence."

"'I think I have radiation sickness,'" quoted Arnold.

"'Me, too,'" said Ardent. "'How about the neighbors?'"

"'There aren't any neighbors,'" groaned Arnold.

"'Well, anyway, we won,'" moaned Ardent.

"'Yes,'" gasped Arnold. "'Aren't you proud?'"

"'We won! We won!,'" chanted Ardent.

"The games affected their view of life itself," continued Ariel. "I watched it carefully. Life — Real Life — is not as serious as the games they made up."

"'Games simulate life,'" quoted Arlene.

"In fact, however," said Ariel, "life is not as purposeful, comprehensible, manageable, definable, learnable, alterable — I mean the rules, now — as the games they made up."

"'Tell me, Sir,'" asked Ardent, "'what is The Object of The Game?'"

"In games, you can answer that question," said Aristo.

"'Capture his king,'" said Arnold.

"'Capture thirteen tricks,'" said Arbutus.

"'Push 'em back, push 'em back. Wayyy — back!'" chanted Arlene and Ardent together.

"In life you cannot define the Object of the Game," said Ariel. "There's no such thing."

"To pile up the most money —" suggested Arnold.

"To be happy with your family —" suggested Ardent.

"To live forever —" said Arbutus.

"To — what?" asked Aristo, perplexed.

"But they tried," insisted Ariel. "And they ended up making life, for them, like their games. The Survival Game."

"'I'm gonna be the last man left,'" said Arnold.

"The Money Game," said Ariel.

"'I'm gonna get more and more, until none of them have any,'" said Arlene.

"The Marriage Game," said Aristo.

"The Dating Game," said Ardent.

"They had 'Playing the Field,'" said Ariel.

Arnold sang, "'Standing on the corner, watching all the girls go by.'"

"They had 'Scoring,'" said Ariel, with scorn.

"'Did you score last night?'" Aristo asked Arnold.

"'He sure did!'" reported Ardent, twisting her body sensuously.

"Think of that," said Ariel. "Copulation, often between persons who didn't really care much about each other, referred to with a term derived from games."

"Their games were a substitute for experience," said Arbutus.

"And life itself became artificial," said Ariel. "Not for real. They were all playing games."

Arnold spoke, as if preaching. "'I tell you, there are no sidelines in the game of life. Everyone is in the game. Some may not be making the most of their opportunity, but they're in the game. No time-outs. No substitutions. No relief for injury. You must continue playing until the game ends.'"

"Utterly absurd," said Ariel. "And the end of them all shows it."

"We aren't sure they really are all gone forever," said Aristo.

"They are," said Ariel. "And I know how it happened. The Scorched Earth Policy was used when armies were retreating across their own country. Burn everything, destroy everything, so the invading army has nothing to conquer but warm cinders. No supplies for the invaders to steal. Leave nothing."

"Their police did that, too, sometimes," said Aristo. "Came looking for illegal substances — whatever *that* meant — and destroyed entire houses."

"That's not quite the same thing," said Ariel. "But it's close. More like this next policy, which was to go far away to save some other country, by destroying everything in it. Kind of a Scorched Earth policy for the Other Guy. It was widely used before the end."

"Like booby-trapping your own house," said Aristo, "so that in case a burglar came in, it blew up your whole house, TV set and sterling silver and all."

"You keep getting ahead of me," said Ariel. "That was the policy that led to the end. They developed a kind of power that would melt or blow to smithereens — everything. Everything! It was like Scorched Earth in advance, and everywhere. They did it very deliberately, but forgot to leave themselves anywhere to retreat to. And then they started the Multiplication Game."

"Another game?" asked Arnold.

"One bunch could destroy the whole earth ten times over," said Ariel.

"Ten times!" exclaimed Ardent. "Whatever for?"

"But the other bunch could destroy the whole world *fourteen* times," Ariel continued. "So, in their scorekeeping state of mind, they claimed they were ahead."

"But in the end —" began Arlene.

"In the end they came to an end," pronounced Arbutus.

Aristo was thoughtful. "It's the first species to be tested that way. Never before did one have to deal with its own capacity to blow up the planet it's living on."

"They failed the cost-analysis test," said Arbutus.

"They knew how to analyze some things, but not others," added Arlene.

"Their analysts did all right," said Aristo. "They announced plainly enough that the price for certain actions and patterns of behavior was extinction."

"'If you pollute the oceans beyond a certain point...'" quoted

Arlene.

"'If you multiply your numbers beyond the food supply...'" quoted Arbutus.

"'If you produce huge masses of radioactivity in the atmosphere...'" quoted Ardent.

"Yet," said Aristo, "they continued doing all of those things. Either they didn't believe their own analysts, or they decided that extinction was the lesser of two evils."

"Ha!" exclaimed Ariel. "They used that phrase to justify a lot of silly things in the last stages. Personally, I think the species was insane, in the end."

"'The end is near!'" chanted Arlene.

◇   ◇   ◇

Ariel confronted Arnold. "And now, I insist we have lunch," he said.

"No!" shouted Arbutus.

Ariel wheeled and threatened her. "Or World War Four!"

"No!" protested Ardent.

Aristo questioned Arlene. "Are you hungry? You look somewhat peak-ed to me."

"How can a black bird look peak-ed?" nagged Arbutus. "She's sick! She'll surely die anyway. So why feed her?"

"No," said Arnold. "She'll revive. I'll go get lunch." And he scooted away.

Arbutus screamed after him. "You're gonna give our precious rations to strangers!?"

"We'll share it," said Ardent, "while there is some. When it's all gone, we'll die loving."

"That is a beautiful philosophy," said Aristo.

"It's pure altruistic stupidity," contradicted Arbutus. "What's the use of surviving *their* stupidity, if we end up dead anyway because of our own?"

"That's what I say!" cried Ardent triumphantly. "Being selfish and nasty and cruel is *stupider* than sharing."

Arnold returned with bowls and a paper sack full of dried corn. "Ahh," said Ariel. "Lunch." He patted Arlene on the back.

"Perk up, Sweetheart. Here comes nourishment."

"I don't see why we're obligated to feed strangers," complained Arbutus.

Arnold handed out bowls, and poured dried corn into each one's bowl. "There are no strangers," he said. "We're all natives here. So let's be friendly. We'll share what we have, as long as it lasts. Something will turn up."

Arbutus examined the contents of her bowl. "Where'd *this* come from?"

Arnold sat and relaxed, and then spoke to Ariel and Arlene. "Sit down. Take it easy. Enjoy. May it do you much good." Then he turned to Arbutus. "It's the seed corn I set aside." He began to eat contentedly.

Arbutus raged. "You're giving away the *seed* corn!?"

"We're sharing it," said Ardent.

"I don't want a fight," explained Arnold. "I like these people. I'm learning things from them. Aren't you, Aristo?"

"Yes," Aristo replied. "They have travelled and observed carefully —"

Arbutus interrupted. "You philosophers will starve to death!"

"It's happened before," Aristo agreed philosophically.

"And because of you, we'll starve, too," wailed his mate.

Arnold chewed and sighed and ignored Arbutus. "Corn is marvelous stuff. It doesn't reproduce by itself. Did you know that? Someone has to help it. *They* used to —"

Arbutus interrupted, shrieking. "Will you stop that irrelevant babbling! If we eat this, what will we do when this is gone?" she demanded.

"I don't know," said Arnold.

"We'll die loving," said Ardent.

"We'll go on learning, meanwhile," said Aristo.

Ariel spoke, seriously. "I want to thank you all. I really didn't want to fight."

"Of course not," said Arnold. "No one's gonna fight." He addressed Arlene. "You feeling any better?"

Arlene perked up somewhat. "Yes, I think so. A little. You

are all very kind."

Ariel was serious. "Maybe you *will* starve because of us."

"Maybe," admitted Arnold, chewing.

Aristo spoke. "Imagine two entities with extremely long life-spans, say, one billion years. One calls out."

"'What was that?'" quoted Arnold.

"'I didn't see anything,'" said Ardent.

"'I saw something flash, but you blinked and missed it,'" insisted Arnold, still quoting.

Aristo explained. "It was a sudden brief increase in the number and activity of a certain species on the planet. Some of the more notable individuals were Lao Tzu, Viracocha, Ramses, Alexander, Hermes, Schweitzer, Heisenberg, Zelda and Blanda."

"'I didn't see anything,'" quoted Ardent.

"You didn't miss much," said Ariel. "They were here and gone in a flash. 'Swoosh,' and they were all gone."

"Too bad," said Arnold. "Some of them were quite remarkable."

"We have come to bury them, not to praise them," said Ariel.

"And we must be smarter than they were," said Arlene.

"How so?" asked Arnold.

"We're here, and they aren't," explained Arlene.

"Yes," said Ariel. "They're gone."

"All you tell us convinces me that it was an accident," said Arnold.

"A preventable accident," said Ardent.

"A preventable accident which isn't prevented is on purpose. I know my logic," said Arbutus.

"Cockroach logic!" countered Arlene.

"Female logic!" suggested Arnold.

"No," said Aristo. "There's only one kind of logic. If it *is* logic."

Ariel spoke to Arnold. "Why an accident? It took a lot of planning and deciding and spending to put that much destructive power in place."

"The fact that we're here means it was an accident,"

explained Arnold. "If it had been done carefully, and deliberately — twenty-four times over — we'd be gone, too." They all froze, and then turned slowly and stared at him for a moment.

Aristo broke the spell. "Imagine a future civilization, a million years from now, gets into archaeology, and starts digging up relics, artifacts of the Old Ones. They come to a huge lead and concrete mass, sealed tight. Labelled, 'Transuranic Waste Depository. Do Not Open.'"

"'Do not open until Christmas,'" quoted Ardent.

"'Do not open for one million Christmases,'" corrected Arbutus.

"But they are obsessed with the need to know," continued Aristo. "'What is it? We don't know. We need to investigate it, and subject it to careful analysis.'"

"'Get it open,'" quoted Arnold. "'Get those crowbars going. Those carbide drills.'"

"'Surprise! Surprise!'" chanted Ardent.

"The radioactive material destroys the new curious civilization," concluded Aristo. "The end of the world. Again."

"The Extermination Game," said Ariel. "They were heavily into extermination."

"Of other folks," said Arlene.

"One kind of extermination leads to another," said Ariel.

"'Is that a passenger pigeon?'" quoted Arbutus. "'I thought we were rid of them. Club it to death!'"

"'I heard someone spotted a whale off Antarctica,'" quoted Arnold. "'But they got it.'"

Arlene seemed to feel better. She said, "You heard about the guy, deeded his body to the cat-food factory --"

"*Cat*-food!" interrupted Ardent.

"He hoped it would save the last of the whales," explained Arlene.

"He was too late," said Arnold.

"And he was a fool," said Arbutus. "How many cans of cat-food can you get from one of them?"

"Several dozen cans," continued Arbutus. "And a whale —

the last whale brings in fifty *thousand* cans!"

"Extermination! But they were after *us!*" cried Aristo. "And we never bothered them at all!"

"'Raid! Raid!'" shrieked Arbutus in mock alarm.

Arlene flapped her wings. "'Black Flag! Beware!'"

"'Roach Motel!'" quoted Aristo. Then he added, "That was after we learned to read."

"They tried to poison us, too," said Ardent seriously. "But they killed many of their own illiterate offspring in the process."

"They thought we were stupid," said Aristo scornfully.

"Yeah," agreed Arlene. "Those scarecrows they used to put up in corn fields never fooled anybody."

"They were absurd," said Ariel.

"But they were also mean," insisted Arlene.

"They talked of survival, while trying to exterminate *us,* and making expensive preparations to exterminate themselves," said Ariel.

"And yet," said Aristo, "The Whole Thing, which includes millions of galaxies, survives."

"Individuals come and go," said Ardent.

"Empires come and go," said Ariel.

"Species come and go," said Arnold sadly.

"Stars," said Aristo, "with their planetary systems, come and go. But *It* goes on and on."

"Or on and off," said Arlene quietly. They all froze, and then turned slowly and stared at her. After a long pause, they all turned again and stared straight ahead.

"I need to think about that," said Aristo at last.

"But we're not finished," complained Arnold.

"I am," said Ariel, getting up. "It's time we got outa here."

"There is no exit," intoned Arbutus.

"Why go?" asked Ardent. "Let's take a nap." She climbed up on the drawer.

"Yes," agreed Arnold. "I need one." He leered at Ardent and climbed up after her. She disappeared into the drawer. Arnold looked back at the others. "Don't you need one?" he asked and dropped into the drawer.

Arbutus backed into the shoe at the toe. Aristo did not stir. "A break from discussion would be fine. I have thinking to do," he said.

Ariel and Arlene looked at each other. He went to the air vent opening. "We need to get outa here," he grumbled.

◇　◇　◇

Two

Sounds of flapping and banging and scratching on metal came down from the air vent. Arlene was inside the vent, calling up. "Ariel! Be careful!"

Arnold stuck his head up out of the drawer, and Aristo appeared at the toe of the shoe. "Can you make it?" called Arlene. "Oh, dear, how will I ever get up there?"

Clattering and scrambling noises came down the air vent. Arnold and Aristo hopped out of their sleeping places. Ardent and Arbutus appeared at the drawer and the shoe. Ariel yelled down from above, "Look out below!"

Arlene backed out of the air vent just as Ariel hit bottom. Arnold trotted over. "You all right?" he asked.

Ariel emerged and brushed himself off. "How can we get outa here?" he asked, sounding angry and a little desperate.

"You can't," said Arbutus smugly, emerging from the shoe.

"So we may as well continue our discussion," added Aristo, rubbing his hands.

"*They* discussed everything," said Arlene.

"I'm sick of them," said Ariel. "Their absurd houses. Weather machines! I want outa here."

"But while you're waiting, let's continue," said Aristo. "You were proving that they were absurd."

"And doing a good job of it, too," said Arlene proudly.

"Yes," agreed Ardent. "They tried to exterminate us, but ended up with a taste of their own medicine."

Ariel turned on Aristo. "Waiting for what?" he asked.

Aristo was silent. "For the door to fall down," answered

Arbutus with scorn. "They all do," she added. "Eventually."
They all froze, and then turned and stared at her for a moment.
At last she said, "Of course, we may starve first."
"C'mon," Arnold asked Ariel. "Tell us more. We'll get you
out soon enough. You've traveled and seen more than we have.
And you're almost as smart as Aristo, here."
"Almost?" bristled Ariel, glaring at Arnold. Then he grinned.
"Very well. I'll trust you, again." He returned to his subject. "I
have plenty more evidence. They blew themselves away in their
absurdity."
"That accident —" began Ardent.
"Absolutely preventable," insisted Arbutus.
"But if they hadn't, they'd have killed themselves with poison
anyway," continued Ariel. "They wanted us to go for it. *They*
liked it so much, and they thought we would, too."
"They filled their food with it," said Arlene. "And their water.
Even their air."
"And it was already hurting them more than it was us,"
concluded Arnold.
"I've been wondering about something," said Aristo. He
turned to Arlene. "Ma'am, are you feeling better?"
"Yes, I am," replied Arlene. "Thanks to your kindness, and
the generosity of all of you. I hope it doesn't mean we'll all
starve —"
"Do you have any idea what made you sick?" persisted Aristo.
"Something she *ate,* no doubt," chimed in Arbutus.
"Something contaminated."
"I'm not sure —" began Arlene.
"Arlene," said Ariel, "it *was* something you ate. In fact, I
warned you."
"What was it?" Aristo asked.
"That corn. Kernels of corn have no business being bright
pink!" Ariel asserted.
"You ate pink corn?" Aristo asked Arlene.
"Yes," she admitted. "I was *so* hungry."
"So," said Aristo, "it wasn't radioactive. What *you* worry

about," he added, nodding to his mate. "It was poisoned. Probably intended for *you* guys," he added, to Ardent.

"Why would anyone be so *mean?*" Ardent wondered.

"Extermination was their big thing, I tell you," said Ariel. "That's why you're sick instead of dead," Aristo said to Arlene. "It was intended for them," and he pointed at the rats.

"Where is this corn?" asked Arnold.

"Down the highway," said Ariel with a shrug. "At the hardware store."

"Is there much of it?" asked Arnold.

"Barrels of it," replied Ariel. "But it's all poisoned."

Arnold jumped up and down and shouted and cheered. "Hooray! Yippee!" He passed out the bowls again and poured more corn form the bag into each bowl.

"Are you crazy?" demanded Arbutus. "What are you doing? We gotta make this last."

"Is *this* poisoned?" Ariel asked suspiciously.

"No," said Arnold. "Our host wouldn't plant poisoned corn. This was his. That stuff at the hardware store only has poison *on* it, intended for us." He leered at Ardent. "But we're too smart for 'em!" To Arlene he added, "Sorry you got sick."

"What are you raving about?" demanded Arbutus.

"We can plant the pink stuff," gloated Arnold. "The poison doesn't affect the new sprouts. We have barrels and barrels of seed corn."

"You were right," Ardent said to her mate with admiration. "You said something would turn up."

"And now we won't have to die loving," said Arnold, hugging Ardent. "Now we can live loving."

"Well, that's fine," said Ariel, sounding not quite sure. He chewed grimly. "There's just one problem."

"What's that?" asked Aristo, sounding almost eager.

"How do we get outa here, to get the corn and plant it?"

Aristo was abashed. "Oh-oh. I shoulda thought of that."

"My philosopher didn't think of something," said Arbutus with disgust.

"Oh, no matter," sang Arnold gaily, skipping a few steps. "We'll solve that problem when the time comes. Meanwhile I wanta hear more of this gentleman's thesis." He stopped in front of Ariel. "They were absurd, you say. They tried to poison us. They almost did poison your mate. Tell us more."

Ariel hesitated and looked Arnold over carefully. Then he blurted, "They believed in magic substances."

"Magic substances?" echoed Aristo with a question.

"'Oh, my splitting headache,'" quoted Arlene.

"'Here, take this stuff,'" offered Arbutus, mocking.

"'Oh, my sore throat is killing me,'" quoted Ardent.

"That faulty respiratory system," Aristo inserted.

"'Here, swallow this,'" offered Arbutus.

"'Oh, my falling feathers, my falling arches, my falling mammary glands, my falling hair —'" lamented Arlene.

"'Here, take this,'" said Arbutus.

"They put magic substances in their food," continued Ariel.

"'This stuff is tasteless,'" complained Arnold, mocking.

"'Here, add this,'" said Ardent.

"'No, not that. This,'" insisted Arbutus.

"'I'll add both!'" said Arnold. He pantomimed adding spices and then ate and savored. "'Aha! That locks the flavor in,'" he murmured.

"'I can't be nursing her very four hours,'" complained Ardent.

"'Try this powdered milk substitute,'" offered Arbutus. "'Just add chlorine — er, I mean, *water*.'"

"They had magic substances that changed their moods and perceptions and thought processes," stated Ariel.

"'Drink this,'" said Ardent to Arnold. "'You'll feel better.'"

"'Ahhh!'" sighed Arnold. "'That's a real picker-upper.'"

Arlene spoke up, quite animated. "Did you hear about the new magic mind-changing substance? It's a downer, really."

"Who would deliberately take in a substance that brought a body down?" asked Arnold.

"Well, maybe not exactly a downer. It just kinda makes ya

kinda stupid," explained Arlene.

"Oh, yes!" exclaimed Aristo. "*That* one. I've heard of it. They had it in the drinking water in all the world capitals."

"'What'll it be for you, Sir?'" Arbutus asked Arnold, imitating someone.

"'Well, Ma'am, I don't drink ethyl alcohol any more,'" Arnold replied, also imitating. "'When I drink alcohol, I become a raging fearless fighting machine. So, I'll have a glass of water. I'll sip it, and we'll all pretend, and no one will get hurt. How much?'"

"'One dollar,'" replied Arbutus.

"'One dollar?'" exclaimed Arnold. "'For a glass of water? Oh, very well. Here.'"

"'Where's the tip?'" demanded Arbutus.

"'Tip?'" echoed Arnold. "'No tip. That *is* the tip.'"

"They made many of these magic substances illegal," Ariel continued.

"Oh," asked Aristo. "So you couldn't get 'em?"

"No," replied Ariel. "So they'd be expensive. They were regulated. You had to buy them at greatly inflated prices from official curers, or official bad-deed-doers, or the police themselves."

"Regulated substance," mused Aristo. "Strange notion! They ate it?"

"Sometimes," replied Ariel. "Or drank it. Or stuffed it up their noses. At other times they set fire to it and breathed in the smoke."

"Didn't it burn their throats and lungs?" asked Arnold in disbelief. They all froze, and then turned slowly and stared at him. At last he continued. "But I suppose they thought it was worth it, to get under the influence that she's always harping about," he added, pointing at Arlene.

"Not exactly," said Ariel. "They ruined throats and tongues and lips and lungs, usually for no reason at all."

"Why would they do that?" asked Aristo.

"I'm demonstrating their absurdity," Ariel reminded him.

"'Why?' is gonna be the wrong question."

Ardent imitated someone. "'Darling, you should quit. That cough. Your grey color. That ugly sore on your lip. Why don't you quit?'"

"'I can't,'" Arnold replied, picking up the charade.

"'You'll have to,'" said Ardent. "'It'll kill you if you don't.'"

"'It'll kill me if I do,'" wailed Arnold.

"Not for some influence that does weird things to your head," continued Ariel, with a glance at his mate. "Just for the fear of what it'll feel like to quit."

"'Stop jiggling like that!'" Arbutus commanded.

"'I'm not jiggling like that on purpose,'" protested Aristo, joining in the imitation. "'I'm nervous!'"

"'Well, get a hold of yourself!'" ordered Arbutus.

"'I can't,'" protested Aristo. "'I told you. I can't quit. I gotta have another one. Maybe I can cut down.'"

"'You been cutting down for ten years,'" nagged Arbutus. "'Now, I say, *quit!*'"

"'I can't,'" insisted Aristo. "'I'll go crazy.'"

"'You'll get cancer,'" threatened Arbutus.

"We *never* had it," interjected Ardent, "until they started giving it to us deliberately."

"I knew one could blow smoke out his ears," said Arnold.

A long pause followed. Ardent was in a private reverie of some kind. She began to moan softly.

"Did you say something?" Arlene asked her.

Ardent woke up. "Oh! Excuse me." She smiled warmly all around. "I was daydreaming. Imagining. Mooning." She leered at Arnold. "Remembering. Getting myself all lathered up."

"Oh," spat Arbutus in disgust. "You mammals are all alike!"

"You can't get serious," said Arlene, agreeing.

"And if you ever *do* get serious," added Aristo, "you can't stay serious."

"Always being distracted," complained Arbutus.

"By your glands!" stated Aristo.

"Ah, yes, glands," sighed Ardent. "Aren't they wonderful!"

"Just wonderful," growled Arbutus. "Simply marvelous."

"Yes," said Ardent. "A rat is only human."

"They *all* were," stated Arlene.

"No," objected Aristo. "Some were not." They were almost mechanical. So thoroughly departmental."

"Well, we cockroaches can reproduce as efficiently as anybody," asserted Arbutus.

"Crows do all right, too," added Arlene.

"Well, so do we," said Arnold. "But aren't you changing the subject?"

"Isn't that what it's for?" asked Ariel.

"Certainly not," said Arnold. "Reproduction may be a result of it, but that's not what it's *for*."

"You're as absurd as they were," Ariel told Arnold. "They reproduced very effectively, somehow, even with their stupid one-at-a-time method."

"*Too* effectively, I've heard," added Arlene.

"But if reproduction has been taken care of adequately, what's all the daydreaming for?" asked Ariel.

"It's so good!" exclaimed Ardent.

"So much fun!" added Arnold.

"That's what most of them thought," admitted Ariel. "I never understood it."

"Oh, but I did," said Ardent.

"They wanted it any time," said Arlene.

"Yes!" said Ardent.

"All the time," added Arlene.

"Yes!" said Ardent.

"In any place," said Arbutus.

"Yes!" said Arnold.

"In any position," added Aristo.

"Yes!" said Arnold.

"Rubbing, stroking," chanted Ardent.

"Throbbing, dripping," chanted Arnold.

"Any and every orifice," said Arbutus with disgust.

"Yes! Yes!" said Arnold and Ardent together.

"That's absurd," concluded Ariel.

"Utterly absurd," added Arlene.

"It is not!" protested Arnold.

"Not at all," insisted Ardent.

◊ ◊ ◊

"How's this for absurdity?" suggested Ariel. "For all their love of sexual activity, of every kind, in every time and place and position, they nevertheless split themselves into two hostile groups, politically, economically and psychologically."

"What two groups?" asked Aristo.

"Men and women," said Ariel flatly.

"'You can't come in the men's locker room!'" shouted Arnold, imitating.

"'Who wants to?'" snarled Arbutus, also imitating.

"'It's a symbol of male superiority,'" Arnold added.

"'Well, you need one!'" sneered Arbutus.

"They made life difficult for those who had most to do with keeping the species going," explained Arlene.

"I thought they were overcoming that particular kind of absurdity," mused Ardent.

"Some of them were working on it," admitted Ariel.

"Some of their men wished the women would take over and be gentle," said Arnold.

"But it was too little, and too late," insisted Ariel.

"And some of their women were not gentle," concluded Aristo. He looked askance at his mate.

"You can't put people into groups and be sure, anyway," said Ardent.

"They sure tried!" exclaimed Ariel. "Groups! It was another of their absurdities. They did all kinds of stupid things because they thought the groups they had defined in their minds really did describe every single member of the groups they had forced every single individual into." The others all froze and then turned slowly and stared at him.

At last Arbutus said to her mate, "The pink ones hired the brown ones to fight us." Then she pointed at the rats. "And them," she added.

"Then they went around bragging that the pink ones were cleaner than the brown ones, because they had less contact with us," said Arnold, sounding puzzled.

"I'm glad they're gone," Arbutus added.

"It's so silly," insisted Aristo. "We knew all along that there was more for us wherever there was waste among them."

"Color had nothing to do with it," said Arlene.

"But they thought it did," explained Ariel. "That's how absurd they were."

"You have to check each time," said Aristo. "Each one is a little different."

"They even had a science of groups," said Ariel.

"'They're dirtier than we are,'" quoted Arlene.

"'They're stupider than we are,'" quoted Aristo.

"'They're sexier than we are,'" quoted Arlene.

"'They have more rhythm than we do,'" quoted Arnold.

"'They're more content with less,'" quoted Arlene.

"'They're more greedy and mean-hearted,'" quoted Arnold.

"'They're more prone to imitate,'" quoted Arbutus.

"'To sing,'" sang Arlene.

"'To swim,'" sang Arnold.

"'To worship trees,'" sang Aristo.

"'To sit in the sun, leaning on a cactus,'" sang Arbutus.

"'To go naked,'" sang Arnold.

"The stupid ones were the ones that wore clothes," asserted Ardent. "Always in the way!"

"Stupid?" questioned Ariel. "Absurd! *Crazy!* Mad!" He pronounced the last word with the flat British "a."

"Mad, mad, *mad!*" echoed Arlene, in the same accent. "Mentally unbalanced," said Arnold.

"Mentally ill," said Ardent.

"Neurotic! Psychotic!" corrected Aristo.

"They named experts who decided who was 'mad' and who wasn't," explained Ariel.

"How could they tell?" asked Arnold.

"They labeled 'crazy' anyone who didn't fit into, or didn't agree to try to fit into, the Reality which the majority defined," Ariel stated.

"'You're outnumbered and outvoted,'" Arbutus said to Arnold, imitating. "'So you're crazy.'"

"'You're odd,'" Arlene added, also to Arnold. "'Strange. Different. Weird. Crazy.'"

"'No!'" screamed Arnold. "'*You're* all crazy!'"

Ariel proceeded. "They built cages for them. Or had special magic substances for them that *really* scrambled their nervous systems, and their glands."

"'Damn you for being different!'" shouted Arbutus at Arnold. "'Take this stuff. And be quiet in your cage.'"

"'Yes, Doctor,'" replied Arnold meekly.

"Often it was the most sensitive and the most logical that were separated out," added Ariel.

"'I don't *want* to work all day and all night all my life,'" complained Arnold, imitating, "'in order to have a big house and two cars and a pick-up and a boat and a cabin in the hills and a lot of letters after my name and a big number beside my name in your computer!'"

"'You're *mad!*'" shouted Arbutus at him. "'Shut up. Take your medicine.'"

"People who tried to figure out their lives were often suspected of being crazy," continued Ariel.

"'Obey me, I say!'" shouted Aristo at Arnold, imitating.

"'But, Daddy,'" protested Arnold. "'I'm almost fifty years old!'"

"'That should have given you time enough to learn to mind your Father,'" Arlene told him, imitating.

"'Well, when do I get to do what *I* want to do?'" whined Arnold.

"'Never!'" retorted Arbutus. "'It's mad to think of such a thing. Take your medicine.'"

"In cases where the whole group was obviously crazy," continued Ariel, "no one noticed. Except to persecute the few sane ones."

"'The war is wrong!'" protested Arnold, imitating. "'The missile system is wicked and preposterous! We're destroying the only place we have! Our favorite planet!'"

"'Shut up,'" ordered Arbutus. "'Go to your cage.'"

"Sometimes going crazy was indistinguishable from going sane," continued Ariel.

"'Oh, poor thing,'" lamented Arlene, imitating. "'Went nuts. Broke up the home. Sued for divorce. Ran off. Disappeared.'"

"'No, my dear,'" contradicted Arbutus. "'Quite the contrary. Went sane. Began to deal with the big questions.'"

"'Who is in control of my life?'" asked Arnold.

"'What do you want?'" Arlene asked him.

"'Who'll do anything about it, if you don't?'" Arbutus asked him.

"The more a person pursued those questions, the crazier he became in the opinion of those who didn't want him to be alive, responsible and free," added Ariel.

"And the children of such a broken home may well have been better off, having one more sane parent than before," said Arlene.

"Blinders were put on them when they were very young," continued Ariel. "By parents, by the group, by the school. Some young ones didn't have them quite in place yet."

Arnold pointed off, imitating. "'The President's New Clothes! He isn't wearing any clothes at all!'"

"A few, too few, parents and teachers tried to warn the young ones," added Ariel.

"'Look out for the blinders!'" called Arlene, imitating.

"Mostly parents were the chief manufacturers and installers of blinders," said Ariel.

"'Here, Kid,'" said Arbutus, imitating. "'Put these on. Wear 'em. Never go out without 'em. Hopefully they'll grow fast to you soon and be permanently stuck on. Never do anything, including thinking and feeling, without these.'"

"Some parents got angry when you took 'em off, no matter

how old you were, or they were," continued Ariel.

"'How dare you disobey me!'" Aristo shouted at Arnold, imitating.

"'It's easier than I thought it would be,'" replied Arnold. "Getting rid of blinders and going sane may have been the same thing," said Ariel.

"'C'mon,'" said Ardent to Arnold. "'Let's play Blind Man's Bluff. You're IT.'"

"'Not me,'" replied Arnold breezily. "'I'm taking these damn blinders off. So I can see. And keepin' 'em off, too.'"

"Going sane looked like going crazy to those who insisted on keeping the blinders on,'" said Ariel.

"'Hey!'" shouted Arbutus, imitating. "'Don't give the game away! Get your blinders back on, like the rest of us.'"

Aristo roused from deep thought and interrupted. "I've been thinking. If your life was being re-run, like on a film or a tape, would this be one of the moments you'd be tempted to switch to 'Fast Forward'?"

"My absurd philosopher," growled Arbutus.

"Or would this be a moment you'd want to slow down?" continued Aristo. "Slow motion. Maybe a still shot. Freeze it and look at it. Hold it a while and really look at it. Study all the angles." They all froze, and then turned slowly and looked at him.

After a long pause, Arlene started up. "Did you hear about the guy, got the idea that the controlled substance he was drinking was causing him permanent brain damage? That stuff makes you think of the damnedest things."

"You should know," snarled Arbutus.

"Went stark raving mad," continued Arlene. "Bananas. Flipped altogether. Had weird echoes in his head ever after. Finally got a job at the Pentagon."

"You're absurd," said Arbutus.

"And let that be a lesson to you all!" concluded Arlene.

Ardent roused from a thoughtful reverie. "You know, when you first meet people, you don't know them very well. Not at all, really. And you think they have no problems. You think they manage their lives better than you do yours."

"So what?" asked Arbutus.

"After you know them better," continued Ardent, "you discover that they have problems. Your respect for their ability to avoid or handle life's problems is in inverse proportion to how well you know them."

"That's marvelous!" exclaimed Aristo. "And stated in such precise mathematical fashion!"

"Check it out," added Ardent coyly.

Arnold addressed Ariel. "Aristo tells me that he's discovered two ways to avoid neurosis."

"What are they?" asked Ariel.

Aristo explained. "The first is to be someone unimportant, someone out of the running for fame or fortune or world-wide acclaim or approval."

"So, I'm safe, then," Arnold interjected.

"You sure are," growled Arbutus.

"People who are important, rich, well-known, famous, who amount to something, who *are* somebody in the group — they're much more susceptible to neuroses than are the ranch hands, the coolies, the Epsilons, and the nobodies," continued Aristo.

"I doubt that," said Ardent. "It's just that some people suffer in silence, and can't afford treatment. What's your other method?"

"Do not care what the neighbors think," intoned Aristo.

"Well, now," said Ariel, "I think you're on to something. Another bit of evidence that they were absurd. They called it 'honor'."

Arnold quoted something to Ardent. "'I could not love thee, dear, so much, loved I not honor more.'"

"'Oh, no,'" wailed Ardent. "'Don't go! Who cares about honor?'" She clutched him close. "'Stay with me!'"

"They cared about what other people, even strangers, would think," continued Ariel.

Arbutus imitated one. "'Darling, be careful. You have your

reputation to think about.'"

"'What will the neighbors think?'" Arlene asked Arnold, imitating.

"'What they wish,'" retorted Arnold. "'They do anyway.'"

"'You mean you don't care what other people think?'" shrieked Arlene. "'You must be crazy!'"

"Actually," added Ariel, "he was sane. But he was also rare. They cared about their image."

"'How do I look?'" asked Arlene, preening, imitating.

"'Oh, I'm so out of fashion!'" lamented Arbutus.

"It hardly matters in the hot tub," interposed Ardent.

"'I'm so out of shape,'" lamented Arlene, imitating.

"Your shape is all right," Arnold told her.

"Listen, Buster," barked Ardent. "What about *my* shape?"

Arnold leered at her. "You know very well how I feel about *your* shape, Sweetheart."

Aristo turned to Ariel. "You're building up quite an impressive case. They *were* absurd."

"Is that enough?" Ariel asked Arnold.

"Enough what?" Arnold asked.

"You delayed feeding us until we laid out more evidence that they were absurd," said Ariel. "Now you delay working on the problem of getting us out of here, so that we can pile up still more. I have proved it, and they are gone. Now can we —"

Ardent interrupted him. "I've been wondering. We do many of the things *they* did. We eat. We discuss things. We reproduce quite efficiently." She leered at Arnold, and then continued. "We try to figure out what's going on."

"So, what are you wondering?" asked Arlene.

"Do you suppose *we're* absurd, too?" blurted Ardent.

"I've wondered about *you,* my dear," growled Arbutus. "You and your marvelous glands —"

"No," interrupted Ardent. "I mean *all* of us. Maybe we're *all* absurd. Maybe everything is absurd. Maybe the Cosmos is absurd."

"No, it isn't," Aristo contradicted flatly. "Some of their really stupid Wise Guys came to that, but the evidence is all the other way."

"*They* were absurd," repeated Ariel. "And it's just like them to accuse the Universe of being absurd instead."

"Yes," agreed Aristo. "It's called projection. Many of them did it."

Arlene imitated someone with a whine. "'Oh, I hate people who go around whining, saying how much they hate people who go around whining, saying they hate people.'"

Arnold imitated someone else. "'The Cosmos makes no sense!'"

"'The Universe is absurd!'" quoted Ardent.

"No!" shouted Aristo. "*That* is absurd. But IT — all of it — is not. You couldn't go to sleep at night, if you thought it was." They all froze, and then turned slowly and stared at him. After a pause, he explained. "Lying down, with the intention of falling asleep, is an act of trust in the Cosmos."

"'What if something absurd happens, while I'm asleep?'" asked Arlene, imitating.

"'Who'll mind the store, while I'm gone?'" asked Arnold.

"'Maybe the sun will burn out, while I'm not paying attention,'" mused Ardent.

"'My effort is what makes the Wheel go round,'" Arbutus asserted. "'The Whole Thing will stop turning, if I stop pushing.'"

Ariel addressed Arnold, both imitating. "'Hey, Cosmos, I'm gonna lie down here in this soft firm warm bed and cover up and go to sleep. You're on your own again for a while. O.K.? I'm taking time out. You take care of things, while I'm gone.'"

"'Sure, Man,'" replied Arnold. "'Where you going?'"

"'Into another reality,'" explained Ariel. "'I need a break from this one.'"

"'Oh,'" said Arnold. "'O.K.'"

"'If there are any problems,'" continued Ariel, "'or slip-ups, or absurdities, I trust you'll know what to do.'"

"'Sure, Man,'" said Arnold.

"'You'll take good care of all the valuable pieces?'" Ariel asked.

"'Of course,'" replied Arnold. "'Relax. Enjoy yourself. Enjoy the pictures. See you when you get back.'"

"The Cosmos is not absurd," Aristo re-affirmed.

"Does the Cosmos have a ruler?" Arlene asked Aristo.

"A ruler?" echoed Aristo.

"A boss. Someone running it. Is anyone in charge?" pressed Arlene. "And if so, who?"

"As if we needed any more evidence of their absurdity," interposed Ariel, "let me tell you that many of them believed that the Universe is an artifact."

"Artifact!" exclaimed Aristo. "Like a broken pot?"

"They thought the whole universe was something that someone else, not part of the Universe, *made!*" continued Ariel. "And that *that* — uh, Being, Entity, whatever — ruled it. Ran it. Made it work."

"How can there be anything outside the Universe?" asked Aristo. "By definition —"

"I know," interrupted Ariel. "*We* all know that, but —"

"By definition," continued Aristo, "the Universe is composed of all that *is*. And there is only one of them."

"Some of their stupider Wise Guys spoke of what they called 'our universe,'" said Ariel.

"*Their* Universe!" exclaimed Arlene.

"As if it belonged to them," continued Ariel.

"Maybe they thought there was more than one," suggested Arnold.

"I've heard of other universes," mused Ardent. "Alternate universes."

"No," said Aristo. "That's the wrong word for that. Other realities, maybe. Other galaxies, no doubt. Other existences made up of anti-matter, or anti-antimatter or anything you like, maybe. But all of *that* —" He waved his arms widely and waxed hot. "All of all of that, whatever it all is, all together, make up *one* thing. *What there is,* the way it is. And there is only one of them. Not two. Not artifact and whatever made it. That's absurd."

"Well," said Ariel with a wry smile, "if that upsets you, wait till you hear this. Many of them believed that that Maker was one of *them!*"

"One of them made the world!?" asked Arbutus, incredulous.

"Well, they made *this* place," said Arnold. "All this stuff —" He waved his hands around the room. "They made *our* world."

"Not just houses and drawers and shoes and air vents," corrected Ariel. "They meant that one of them made the mountains and rivers and planets and suns and space and time."

"They believed that one of them made all the galaxies and the anti-matter realities and — everything?" squealed Ardent.

"It is utterly absurd," asserted Aristo. "They, if there are any left, have only been in existence as long as the light we see from the nearest galaxy takes to get here."

Ardent spoke to Aristo. "Try that again, please."

"All right," said Aristo. "We look at the Andromeda galaxy. It's the nearest of billions. What we see is light that left there before any of *them* existed at all. We cockroaches are much older, to be sure, but we aren't claiming that some cockroach made the world!"

"That *would* be absurd," said Arlene quietly.

Aristo became more excited, and a little cross. "No more so than to say that one of *them* did. It's not absurd. It's preposterous! And an insult to all the other galaxies!"

"Take it easy, Aristo," said Arnold.

"Let's just discuss it," agreed Ardent.

"O.K.," said Aristo. "Our galaxy, The Milky Way, is so small that, viewed from other galaxies that we can see, we would be invisible. We can see them, but they can't see us, because we're too small. This is by comparing widths of galaxies."

"Do tell," said Arlene.

"Our galaxy is in a sparsely settled neighborhood," continued Aristo. "Most of the action is somewhere else. We are in the New Mexico of the cosmos. It's a pleasant place to be. It has charm and beauty and is a good place to raise kids, but elections and decisions are determined elsewhere. Nothing in this galaxy *made* the Whole Thing. *Nothing* made the Whole Thing. Who would have made the Maker?"

"Their children asked that and were shushed for being impudent," added Ariel.

"The Cosmos is *one,* not Two!" shouted Aristo.

"Well, my dear philosopher," said Ariel, "try some of these other propositions, while you're at it."

"'The King of the Universe wants one group to kill every last man, woman and child of the other group,'" asserted Arlene, quoting something.

"'The King of the Universe wants the population of his species to multiply geometrically indefinitely,'" quoted Arbutus.

"'The King of the Universe made them male and female and made them attractive to each other and then declared it wrong for them to act upon that attraction,'" quoted Ardent.

"'The King of the Universe wants most of his species to boil in oil in eternal conscious torment, as punishment for breaking laws most of them never heard of,'" quoted Arbutus.

"'The King of the Universe wants all evergreen trees slaughtered on the anniversary of his birthday,'" quoted Arnold.

"'The King of the Universe died,'" stated Arlene.

"'The King of the Universe saves most retail outlets from bankruptcy annually on the occasion of his birthday,'" affirmed Arbutus.

"'Getting drunk on the freeway is the most commonly known method of celebrating the birth of the illegitimate son of the daughter of the moon,'" intoned Arlene.

"'That nice one in the red suit with the flying deer separates the sheep from the goats and distributes the results of year-end retail sales,'" stated Ardent.

Ariel patted Aristo on the back. "How about that?"

"It's — absurd," acknowledged Aristo.

"I'm wondering about something, again," said Ardent thoughtfully.

"What is my gorgeous glandular sweetheart wondering now?" asked Arnold.

"Talk, talk, talk," said Ardent. "Words, words, words. *They* did a lot of that."

"They often hid from problems behind walls of words," agreed Ariel.

"Are *we* doing it?" asked Ardent. "Why do we have language? What for?" They all stared at her. "To hide behind? To prevent our feeling our feelings? Little jokes, or massive dissertations, instead of —" She paused. The others waited, watching her intently. "When a touch of the hand on someone's arm, or a pat on the shoulder, or a bear hug, or a tear, or gut-wrenching sobs and slobbering weeping and gasping would really be more appropriate."

"Talk, talk, talk," echoed Arlene. She spoke directly to Ardent. "I see what you mean."

"We're verbal," said Ardent. "But is there a risk of getting *too* verbal?"

"They were," stated Ariel.

"We talk about it," said Ardent, "instead of feeling it, or doing it — whatever it is that needs feeling or doing."

"Sometimes they talked themselves out of what needed doing," stated Ariel.

"Sometimes it's a wall of words," continued Ardent. "It comes at you continuously, an unending flow of styrofoamy mush that absorbs or fends off all suggestions, hints, probes, barbs, bullets — an impenetrable wall of words which protects the manufacturer and user from ever feeling whatever it is that is going on, and prevents his or her doing much about it beyond the incessant talk, talk, talk." She paused and they waited. "Are we doing that?" she asked quietly.

"I don't think so," said Aristo finally. "What we're saying is important."

"I think you're making *me* do it," said Ariel.

"How?" asked Arnold.

"I want to get out of here, but you all want to talk. And I'm letting you suck me into talking, talking, talking, instead of working on the problem." They all froze, and then turned slowly to stare at him.

◇   ◇   ◇

"There's another thing they did with language which we need to be aware of," said Aristo.

"What's that?" Arnold asked the cockroach. Then he turned to the disgusted bird and said, "We'll tend to your problem, Ariel. I promise. Be patient."

"They used words," said Aristo, "not to tell what they knew, or how it seemed from their individual angle, or how it felt. They used language to deceive each other."

"How?" asked Arnold.

"They said things that weren't so," Aristo stated.

"Oh," said Arnold. "They made mistakes."

"Yes, they did," agreed Aristo. "Plenty. But I don't mean that. They deliberately said things that they knew weren't true, even as they said them."

"Yes," said Ariel. "And now we're on beyond absurd."

"If you lie once," said Arbutus, "you lose your truth virginity, and are a liar."

"Their presidents and cabinet secretaries and ambassadors and news reporters did it all the time," asserted Arlene.

"They lied about everything," said Ariel. "They said they wanted peace, but they did not."

"They had the gift of language, and used it to confuse each other," lamented Ardent. "That's terrible."

"Maybe they lied even to themselves," mused Aristo.

"I think this is the most unique thing about them," said Ariel. Then he quoted something. "'This is the species that lies. Our messages are unreliable.'"

"One of their Wise Guys had the notion that Truth would overcome their tendency to lie," stated Arbutus.

Arnold turned to her. "I didn't know *you* studied philosophy, too," he said.

"*All* cockroaches are philosophers!" she asserted.

"Well, reassure me about Truth," Ardent said to her.

Arbutus continued. "He said that Truth can never be told so as to be understood, and not be believed."

"So," said Ariel, picking it up, "if you find someone not believing you, either —"

"You didn't tell it right," offered Arlene.

"Or —" continued Ariel.

"He didn't understand it right," said Arnold proudly.

"*or* —" continued Ariel, raising his voice.

"It isn't true!" concluded Ardent.

"I'm not so sure," said Aristo thoughtfully. "Truth may be too big and too complicated for us *ever* to tell it, or understand it, completely right."

"It sure seems that way to me," agreed Arnold. "But, then, I'm not as smart as all of you." They all froze, and then turned slowly and stared at him.

Ariel finally spoke, grimly and with a little menace. "You better be smart enough to get us out of here!"

"There is no way out," chanted Arbutus. "No exit."

"We'll eat the last of that corn and die loving," said Ardent.

"No," said Arnold.

"Maybe one of them will come," mused Aristo.

"There are none of them left," stated Arlene.

"The door will fall down, eventually," asserted Arbutus.

"I'll get us out," said Arnold.

"You know a way out?" Ariel asked him.

"I'll show you. Later. First, I gotta add a little more to our discussion," said Arnold.

"Why?" Ardent asked him. "Show him now. Then you can talk all you want to. He's been pretty patient."

"Once they're out they may just keep on going," said Arnold. "Let me tell 'em this first."

"O.K.," said Ariel. "But talk fast, Buster."

"Don't be impudent," snarled Arbutus. "We fed you."

"You were all very generous," interposed Arlene. "What is it, Arnold?"

"I have to say that there were some things that they did that I liked," said Arnold. "I even miss them!"

"How can you miss liars and exterminators?" Arlene asked.

"Yes, exactly what do you miss?" questioned Ariel.

"Music," said Arnold.

"And what is music?" asked Aristo.

"Uh —" began Arnold, and then he hesitated. "Uh, tones. Beats. Songs." He began singing. "'We're waltzing in the wonder of why we're here...'"

"I used to hear them do that and I never understood it," said Arbutus. "Did it while they washed themselves. A special method of spitting and caterwauling."

"Wasn't that the same racket that rattled the windows and air ducts?" asked Arlene. "All that banging and thumping?"

"What does it do?" Aristo asked Arnold.

"It doesn't *do* anything," he replied. "It, uh — means things. Sometimes. Not always. It —" He stalled. "I don't know. I liked it." He sang again, leering at Ardent. "'Darling, we are growing old...'"

"You aren't explaining it very well," said Aristo with a tone of disgust.

"If you ask me," said Ariel, "it's another sign that they were absurd. You may be, too," he added to Arnold.

"No," said Arnold flatly. "Music had the rhythms of life, of existence. It had passion —"

"Passion!" exclaimed Ardent. "You mean that throbbing —"

"Throbbing, pulsing, beating in rhythm —" said Arnold. "And pattern. The pattern of the Cosmos." He sang again. "'What the world needs now, is love, sweet love...'"

"He's as absurd as they were," Ariel told the others.

Arlene became manic again. "You heard about the jazz fanatic, used to love to swing and stomp and clap and sway in time to the music. Said he felt he was right *inside* the music. Another fellow asked him, one time," and she turned to Arnold, quoting, "'What's that song they're playin'?'"

Arnold swayed and hummed and shifted his weight from one

foot to another. "'Oh, no tellin'!'" he answered. "'It's jazz, ya know, and with jazz, if you recognize what it *is,* they ain't playin' it right!'"

"Totally absurd," growled Arbutus. "Thumping and plunking and plinking and clinking and screeching and squeaking and clattering and howling and whining and —"

Ardent interrupted and continued. "And keening and panting and sighing and growling and groaning and gasping."

"No meaning to it. Nothing but pattern," said Ariel.

"The patterns of life," agreed Arnold, still swaying.

"The patterns of the Cosmos," said Aristo.

"Some of them cared about — all that," said Arnold.

"Well, it doesn't matter," said Ariel. "They're gone now."

"They did another thing," said Arnold. "I used to watch it and enjoy it. I really miss it."

"I don't see how you can miss such an absurd and dangerous species," asserted Arbutus.

Arnold continued, ignoring her. "They used to go to special places for the music. And sometimes in those special places, they'd watch each other pretending."

"Pretending what?" asked Aristo.

"Different things," explained Arnold. "They'd pretend each one was someone, or something, else. They'd act out make-believe lives."

"Better lives than their real ones?" Aristo asked.

"Sometimes," said Arnold. "Not always. Just different. Imaginary."

"Didn't they have real lives to live?" asked Aristo.

"Maybe *that*'s what ailed them," suggested Ardent. "They were only pretending to be alive."

"Why would they pretend?" asked Arlene.

"Maybe they were trying to understand what might happen in certain situations," suggested Arnold.

"Or maybe they wanted to remember something that happened earlier," suggested Ardent.

"Maybe they wanted to forget," suggested Arlene. "Forget

how mean and thoughtless and senseless they really were."

"I don't know," admitted Arnold. He hesitated before continuing. "I have to tell you this. Some of the imaginary scenes they went to see made no sense. They were absurd."

"You didn't understand them," said Aristo.

"They didn't understand them, either," said Arnold. "They all said so. There was nothing to understand."

"But they kept on going to see them, and said they were marvelous, and said that they liked them?" asked Ardent.

"The truth of the absurdity of what they were doing to themselves was too painful, so they distracted themselves with additional deliberate absurdities," stated Arbutus.

"It was even more complicated than that," said Arnold. "Some of them had the idea that others of them ought not to see or hear certain of these imaginary scenes."

"Even the scenes that were absurd?" asked Aristo.

"Yes," said Arnold.

"How can you censor absurd things?" asked Aristo. "It has to make sense first. Then it has to be a sense that someone doesn't like."

"No sense at all can hardly be objected to," agreed Arbutus. "Except as a waste of time."

"Does this make sense?" asked Ardent.

"This what?" Arlene asked her.

"Does The Whole Thing make any sense?" Ardent asked. They all froze and then turned slowly and stared at her.

After a long pause Ariel said, "I don't believe it does."

"I can't tell," said Arlene.

"I do believe it does," said Aristo.

"I don't know," said Ardent.

"I'm not sure it does, but I want it to. A philosopher is only human," said Arbutus.

"I know it doesn't, but I keep testing it as if it did," added Ariel.

"It seems to me it might make a kind of sense," said Arnold, "but we don't know what that sense *is*. I think we all hope it does. We all want it to."

Arlene started her manic thing again. "Did you hear about the guy, made up imaginary scenes, for the others to read or go watch? Wrote 'em down. Good ones. Not absurd ones. The kind that made folks think seriously about life. No one paid any attention to him or his imaginary scenes. No one would read his stuff or look at his scenes."

"That's another form of censorship," injected Aristo.

"Guy keeps trying," said Arlene. "At first his wife believes in him. Says the stuff is good. Supports him. Works hard in a factory every day, and pays the bills for both of 'em. But after several years she loses faith in him and his work."

"'It's pure crap!'" spat Arbutus. "'You're wasting my time! *I'm* wasting my time!'"

"And she left him," continued Arlene. "He had to go to work, and couldn't write any more unread and unwatched imaginary scenes."

"Maybe some good stuff got away," mused Aristo.

"It *all* got away!" shouted Ariel. "Remember? They blew themselves and all their ideas and all their imaginary crap all away. Away, away, *away!*" He waved his wings frantically.

"And let that be a lesson to you all!" concluded Arlene, but this time she didn't droop.

Arnold spoke to Ariel. "O.K., my friend. Come with me." They trotted off together. The others could still hear Arnold. "Push on this. With me. On three." They could hear sounds of straining and grunting. "One, two, *three!* Push!" They heard more grunting and a scraping sound. "Look out!" yelled Arnold. "Get back!" The others heard a loud crash of something heavy and wooden, falling and reverberating. Then silence. Then the long drawn-out sound of a very squeaky door opening.

The group scampered toward the sound. "What happened?" called Ardent. "Are you all right?"

Arnold met them. "We're fine," he assured them.

"What fell?" asked Aristo.

"A prop," said Arnold. "We moved it."

"And the door opened?" Aristo asked. They all looked, marvelling at the huge opening in The Kitchen. The Back Door stood wide open. "Marvelous," said Aristo. "Brilliant engineering."

"Where's Ariel?" asked Arlene.

"He went out," said Arnold.

"Ariel!" shrieked Arlene. "Wait for me!" She trotted out the open door.

"I hope they come back," said Arnold.

"Surely they'll say goodbye," said Ardent.

Aristo spoke to Arnold. "How long have you known about that door?"

"Quite a while," said Arnold. "It never occurred to me that you'd be interested."

"You didn't set that prop yourself," Aristo said dubiously.

"Oh, no," replied Arnold. "*They* did. But I watched."

Arlene and Ariel came back in through the open door.

"So, you found a way out?" said Ardent warmly.

"Yes," said Ariel. "Arnold did. We wanted to say 'thank-you.'" He offered his hand to Aristo, and they shook all around.

"You'll be leaving?" Arnold asked the crows.

"Yes," Ariel replied. "We need open air."

"If you find some of them, come tell us," said Arnold.

"What makes you think we might find any of them?" asked Ariel.

"If we survived, maybe some of them did," said Arnold. "Some of the kind that aren't proud. Or mean. Or absurd."

Ardent spoke to Arlene. "Will you go far?"

"No," Arlene answered. "We're needing a nest. That mulberry bush in the yard will do fine, I think."

"Oh, good!" gushed Ardent. "You have glands, too. I'll come visit. I *love* babies!"

Arnold shook hands with Ariel. "Thanks for the visit. Let's talk again, soon." The birds strolled out, arm in arm, waving at the others. "Goodbye!" shouted Arnold.

Ardent climbed up on the drawer and then turned and looked back down at Arnold. "I'll be right up, Sweetheart," he called to her.

Arbutus backed into the shoe. Arnold spoke to Aristo. "Nice folks."

"Yes," said Aristo, but he was distracted. "I have a great deal of thinking to do." He crouched down next to the toe of the shoe and ignored Arnold.

"See you after a while," said Arnold, climbing up onto the drawer. "We can talk about it later." Aristo was lost in meditation and did not reply. Arnold dropped into the drawer.

◊   ◊   ◊

On Satire — an Afterword

My Dear Muse,

This is to protest your laying on me the most difficult writing task there is — satire. You fill me with a kind of moral indignation, about pretense and phoniness and lying in high places, and you combine that with an average or better awareness of what is going on in the world. You taught me to love to read. You gave me a working sense of humor. You let me walk in other people's moccasins, at least a little. You awakened in me an imagination and it survived the disastrous training of my childhood and youth. You force me to think that I can make up stories, to account for what I observe, although "critics" have tossed the stories aside, calling them "parables." I don't mind so much your insisting that I write parables — it's an old and venerable tradition which includes Nathan, Aesop, Jesus, Boccaccio, Bunyan, Twain and Shaw.

The school of satirists features my most highly regarded model of all, Jonathan Swift. No one ever did it, or will ever do it again, better than he. And he feels so contemporary! More than two and a half centuries ago he dealt definitively with lawyers, doctors, government bureaucrats, doublespeak, militarism and science. Instead of trying to write more satire, I sometimes think I should find a way to require all my potential readers to go back and read and memorize *GULLIVER'S TRAVELS*. But you won't let me off that easily.

And it is becoming more and more difficult, whether you know it or not. You are aware that Tom Lehrer gave up satire, which he was very courageous in wielding and had become very good at. He first made us aware of "Pollution," and the need for "lead B.V.D.'s," and the shame of religion for sale, and the folly of American militarism and nuclear proliferation. He says he quit on the day that Henry Kissinger, one of the greatest war criminals of this century, was awarded the Nobel Peace Prize. You can't make a satire out of that kind of reality. It's already satire.

My work becomes more difficult all the time. The reality seems to come at us pre-packaged in the form of satire already. For example:

[1] The Department of Energy promises to keep radioactive material "out of the environment" for 10,000 years. But consider:

[a] There is no place "out of the environment" — outer space is still in the environment.

[b] Ten thousand years ago was before the invention of agriculture.

[c] Language changes, almost to incomprehensibility, every 500 years; 10,000 years is twenty times that.

[d] The material that we need to be protected from will still be lethal after 250,000 years.

[e] The government is making, and allowing power companies to continue to make, still more of this material.

[2] The ozone layer, which shields the earth's surface from harmful cosmic radiation, is deteriorating, thanks to human use of a series of chemicals that do not occur free in nature. But consider:

[a] The U.S. government refuses to join a world-wide ban on those chemicals.

[b] Members of Congress mock the scientists who are unanimous in their agreement about this menace.

[c] Chemical companies resist proposed laws which would ban the chemicals ten years from now.

[d] Millions for research for "cures," but not one cent for "prevention," is the current motto.

You make it very difficult. Attempts to make jokes about leukemia result in what is called "bad taste." It becomes nothing better than, "Well, Mrs. Lincoln, besides *that*, how was the play?"

"Environmentalists," and I guess I'm one, are labeled "a special interest group." And you want me to make that seem funny! Isn't it already patently ridiculous? Isn't *everyone* an environmentalist? Can it be that only a "special interest group" cares about the survival of the Biosphere, while the rest are busy profit-taking? So, I'm laughing. It only hurts when I laugh.

Your power over me, O Muse, is absolute, I realize. I cannot desist. Thanks to you I cannot and will not shut up. But I want you to know that your demands are verging on the unreasonable.

◇ ◇ ◇

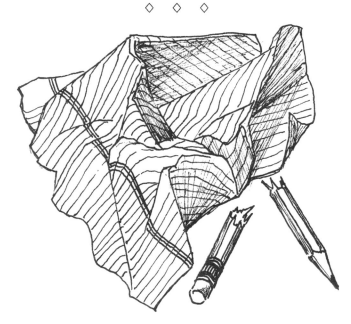

DUKE CITY TALES
STORIES FROM ALBUQUERQUE
by Harry Willson
ISBN: 0-938513-00-0 [176 pp. $9]
Illustrated by Claiborne O'Connor

Luminarias, balloons, atomic bombs, bats, false arrest, hunting, finding, moonwatching, DWI, cops, schools, litter, mufflers, stray dogs, and a fumbling old alchemist, who attempts to use his occult powers to bring about his goal of "peace and quiet," with results that are comical and less than satisfactory, giving pause to those of us who feel called upon to change the world.

"Duke City" is Albuquerque -- the commercial, educational, medical, military metropolis that contains half the population of New Mexico. Harry Willson, has lived there more than thirty-five years as a practicing mythologist and story-teller.

"Willson's keen insight into human nature is intermingled cleverly within the stories' events, revealing both the stupid and the serious, the touching and the absurd, leaving the reader feeling that he has just been exposed to a truth that he has sensed before, but which for the first time is verbalized." -- THE SMALL PRESS REVIEW

"...a nice mix of stories for students and adults alike... a real sense of environmental need... If you could change the world, how would you do it? ...a light touch of humor... creative tales and endearing characters." -- THE NEW MEXICO ENGLISH JOURNAL

"...a striking shift away from contemporary fiction's usual assumption that violence, oppression and injustice are somehow 'natural.' ...Willson keeps reminding us that it's O.K. to believe in peace." -- PLOWSHARES PRISONER

"...a series of vignettes about modern life in the Sun Belt with a quiet sort of intimacy. This book will be of great interest to anyone curious about contemporary Southwest fiction." -- THE BLOOMSBURY REVIEW

THIS'LL KILL YA
and Other Dangerous Stories
by Harry Willson
ISBN: 0-9622937-2-5 [184 pp. $6]

A purposely exaggerated spoof on censorship, the title story is a murder mystery in which the chief suspect is a book! Censorship Committee, beware! How can you censor it without reading it? And this is the book, that, if ya read it, it'll kill ya. The other stories here are the sort that censors would obliterate, if they could.

CAUTION! READING THIS BOOK MAY BE HAZARDOUS TO YOUR HEALTH!

"There's something to outrage everyone, ranging from conjugations of certain Anglo-Saxon "magic words," to explicit sex, violence and attacks on religion and science. ...No author I've read since John Steinbeck has written with such great love for the world, and such a profound sense of humor."
-- J. G. Eccarius, IDEAS AND ACTION

"Willson's striking stories deftly combine apocalyptic global vision with robust down-home wit. This'll make you smile, and his humor'll make you think."
-- Gene H. Bell-Villada, author & critic, Williams College

"The policeman investigating his book is, naturally, a bit cautious once he gets his hands on a copy of the loathsome and fearful volume. The reader also tends to become cautious, after a while, since it soon becomes obvious that the book you are reading is the book you are reading about -- the book that can kill people, which is called THIS'LL KILL YA. Fortunately, the book will only kill you if you share the most common superstition in our culture -- the idea that words on paper can be dangerous... The more deeply you fear certain ideas, images and taboo topics generally, the more likely it is that the book, THIS'LL KILL YA, might in fact kill ya."
-- Robert Anton Wilson, TABOO: THE ECSTASY OF EVIL

"A dogma-busting story about a subversive little book and its effect on different people. An enjoyable book that contains some humorous gems."
-- bOING bOING

"...political, social and environmental commentary and satire that is seen much too infrequently these days... Willson shows himself to be a bold, uncompromisingly honest, yet humorous writer, about the ills of today's society... Provoking insights, not only about censorship and its effects, but about the nature of humanity, intelligence and life itself... He leaves us pondering how unprepared and unprotected we are, and the value systems that it seems must be implemented if we are to survive at least some of the messes that we have allowed ourselves to be set up for."
-- Caroline Ravenfox, THE SUN, Santa Fe, NM

AMADOR PUBLISHERS
P. O. Box 12335
Albuquerque, NM 87195
505-877-4395
To Order: 800-730-4395

ORDER BLANK

of copies   price

____VERMIN   @ 10.00_____
____CHRISTMAS BLUES   @ 15.00_____
____DUKE CITY TALES   @ 9.00_____
____A WORLD FOR THE MEEK @ 9.00_____
____SOULS AND CELLS
              REMEMBER   @ 8.00_____
____THIS'LL KILL YA   @ 6.00_____
____THE LITTLE BROWN
              ROADRUNNER   @ 4.00_____

              Subtotal_____

      Shipping [$2.50 per order]_____

              Total, enclosed_____

Send to: Name_____

      Address_____

      City, State, Zip_____